GW00792392

365 Days of Inspiration

365 Days of Inspiration

365 Days of Inspiration
© David Salmon

Book cover photograph and design:
Jaquetta Trueman, Graphic Solutions

First published in 2006 by Ecademy Press
ISBN Number 1-905823-04-5 (978-1-905823-04-8)

Contact:
Ecademy Press
6, Woodland Rise
Penryn, Cornwall, UK
TR10 8QD
info@ecademy-press.com

Printed and Bound by Lightning Source UK and USA

Welcome to 365 days of inspiration

My Mission

To release the empowerment within individuals enabling them to be inspired and to unlock their own inspiration which creates
the reality they desire.

David Salmon - Writer, Publisher and Speaker

This book is dedicated to:

Martine Delamere for her insight and giving me strength to make many changes

George Metcalfe for his wisdom and support

Nigel Risner for stretching me and daring me to make the changes I never thought possible

Topher Morrison for daring me to dream

To my children Anthony, Anna, and Emma who have given me inspiration and make me very proud

I hope you enjoy this book of inspiration as much as I did in putting it together

David Salmon

Foreword

Here is an intensely powerful book of encouragement and inspiration. It will raise your game and help you find the right level of enthusiasm to move forward each day .

Set out in an "action planning diary" form it enables you to plan and take regular action for yourself. There are two specially chosen inspirational or thought provoking quotations for each . Some of these David Salmon has collected over the years as having affected him profoundly. Many of the others he has composed himself.

David is a man of action. He has long recognised the practical value of self-development. As his coach I have been witness over the years to his steely determination to build a successful business. But I have also been privileged to have been allowed to share his growing interest in a more spiritual life-balanced existence and his desire to share this with other people.

This book is David Salmon's unique way of demonstrating that with determination and (some humility) you really can "have it all".

Read this book. Work with it each day. Have fun and watch yourself grow.

George Metcalfe

Are you looking for inspiration?

Welcome to **YOUR** 365 days of inspiration

We all need food and nourishment in order to survive.

What kind of inspiration do **you** feed yourself in order to be inspired enabling **you** to achieve **your** goals and to live an abundant life?

365 days of inspiration is not just a book giving you inspiration for every of the year, it is very much a journey.

A way of life to create for **yourself,** a relationship between yourself and the book, enabling the book to become alive and much more.

When I started to write the book I was thinking of providing one important inspiration thought for each day, which would have been a valuable pocket sized book, but then I changed my mind, **you** deserve more and I decided to give you TWO thoughts for each ; one in the morning and one for the evening. WOW that's 730 thoughts to nourish and inspire you with.

You can start immediately and you will unlock the inspiration within yourself.

By purchasing 365 days of inspiration not only will you receive inspiration every , you will also receive the following benefits:

GOALS   How to create goals, how to turn dreams
                         into goals and how to turn goals into
                         reality. By using these techniques you will
                         then turn your 365 days of inspiration into
                         a working program to create, visualize
                         and achieve your goals

AFFIRMATIONS What is an affirmation? How do they

work for you? Creating your own affirmations. By using affirmations you will be able to fast track your way to achieving your goals

SUCCESS LOG   Working on your successes. As we all go though life reading the newspapers or watching TV, we are mainly fed with negative news. Therefore it is not surprising that we feel down most of the time. However by using the success log program you are able to use the 365 days of inspiration to record your successes and to be able to acknowledge those successes that you have achieved.

FREE GIFT

My FREE gift to you will be a regular newsletter every two weeks providing you with even MORE inspirational quotes and information building on the foundations of your 365 days of inspiration.

So let's start

There is a thought for the morning and one for the evening. So why not write the morning thought down each and carry it around with you or put it on a post-it note on the fridge, on your desk, etc. Just remind yourself of the thought during the day, and then in the evening take a look at the second thought of the and focus on it during the evening. Just regard this as part of your normal exercise regime and get into the habit of reviewing your thoughts each . Just think, each your inspirational thoughts are building and getting strong, and by the end of this journey of 365 days you will have 730 thoughts that you can draw upon.

That's all very well.

But I want to give you much more.

You will notice that each page has a number of sections which are blank for you to build on your inspiration:

My goal for today

My affirmation for today

My successes for today have been…

More food for thought…

Let's START with:

GOALS

There are several books and courses on goal setting and here are a few thoughts that work for me.

A goal must have a beginning and an end to be achievable and needs to fulfill certain criteria.

For a GOAL to be qualified, have a look at the SMART method

S is for specific

M is for motivational

A is for achievable

R is for realistic

T is for time base

Let's have a look at those in more detail:

Specific
The usual response to what is your goal is "I want more money" or

"I want to be financially independent". This is too vague. How much money exactly do you feel that you need? Is it $10,000 or $100,000 or $1,000,000 ,what's the exact figure? Be sure to be specific and to recognize what it means to you and what effect and benefit it would have for you (don't forget you can have lots of money and riches and still be unhappy).

Motivational

When setting the goal what is going to motivate and drive you to take the steps to achieve it? An example of this would be "I would like to run a marathon". Great goal, but what is going to motivate you to achieve it - if you have a burning desire to get fit and/or raise money for charity that will motivate you . No matter how many goals you set, large or small, unless you have the motivation, a passionate desire, you won't get started, let alone achieve the end result.

Achievable

Is it achievable? Let's take the two examples above. Is it achievable to earn $100,000, with the question has it been done before? The answer is YES, you just need to start to make the step to achieve it. Could you run a marathon as long as you are fit and can dedicate time to training? Again the answer is yes, subject to taking certain actions. Most things are possible and achievable, but be realistic.

Relevant

How relevant is your goal to you and your desires? Running a marathon may sound a good goal but how important is it to you? Again it's back to passion and desire. What feeling will it create for you?

Time based

A goal must have a begining and an end. It is no good to say I want £100,000 next year or I want to run a marathon next year, because next year never arrives. You need to be time based, "by 1st July 2006 I will have £100,000 in my bank account" or "on the 1st May 2006 I will have completed the "XXXX" marathon."

Always give clear instructions for your goals:

Do you really, really want it?
Can you see it?
Can you see yourself in the picture?
As Napoleon Hill said "you need to conceive to achieve"

Don't keep your goals a secret, share them with others, they will then be able to support you in achieving your goals.

It is also important to visualize your goal, create a goal book or goal picture board for your room. If your goal is to have a certain type of car, then get pictures of it and put them on your board. If it is to visit a certain holiday resort or destination, then again get pictures of it and again put them on your board. Give yourself every opportunity to visualize your goal within your inspirational mind.

AFFIRMATIONS

So what is an affirmation? It is a strong, positive statement telling us that all is well, to enable you to move forward. It can be a very powerful tool helping you to push through even the worst of your fears. Affirmations become very powerful when created in the present tense. For example I am creating an abundant life, instead of I will create an abundant life. The former says we are already making it happen and creating the process of inspiring your life.

If you say affirmations often enough you will ultimately believe them, you will find that the more you repeat them your interaction with the outside world and your reaction to problems will change.

Aim to say your affirmations out loud every at least 10 times. This will reinforce them in your mind.

Another tip is to always state affirmations in the positive - such as I am self-confident rather than I am lacking in confidence.

Affirmations are different to goals in that they do not need to be too specific. They are there to put things into perspective and enable you to trust yourself. You will need to experiment to find what works for you, but here are a few ideas to get you started.

For purpose   I matter and act as if I do
                             I spread love wherever I go

For self respect I take responsibility for my life
                             I am great
                             What ever happens I can handle it

For Trust   I am relaxed and allow my life to unfold
                             I trust and can let go

For gratitude   I find good in all experiences
                             I recognize my many blessings

I hope you get the picture, but just in case here are my own affirmations that I use:

It's all happening perfectly

I am powerful and loving and I have nothing to fear

I am creating a wonderful abundant life

I can't lose regardless of the outcome of the decisions I make

I'll handle it

I say these affirmations out loud to my self each morning and again at night, 10 times each. But please work on your own for yourself.

By using the 365 day journal you will be building and reinforcing your own affirmations every . No excuses please!

Success log

How often when we reflect on the and speak to friends and partners do we talk about all the things that are negative or have gone wrong? "I missed the train, "I didn't get everything done".

Why not create a success log to acknowledge everything that has gone right and to congratulate yourself.

When asked to name 50 successes, most people will struggle because they will be looking for big successes in their life like " I got married on... my child was born on... I got a new job on ... I got a new car" and so on but when looking at our goals in order to achieve them we need to take a number of steps at a time. Sometimes we take several steps over a period of time and it is important to record, recognize and look back on achievement which you may not have recognized before.

What do I mean? Here's just a few taken from my own journal over the past few weeks:

I wrote down my goals for the next 3, 6 and 12 months.

I listened to my new music CD

I completed on my investment property purchase

I met a new client

I watched my daughter playing hockey

I went for a 60 mile cycle ride

I paid my credit card bill

I spoke to Judy

I did my accounts

I had a great picnic on the beach

I registered my domain name Inspiration4 me.com

These are just ten taken at random over the past few weeks, and every night I take my journal and look to acknowledge and record ten successes for that , both personal and business/work, large and small.

Please try it for YOURSELF

By using 365 days of inspiration you will be able to record 5 successes for each . Just think, that's over 1800 successes that you will be able to look back on when you get to the end of the book.

More food for thought

This is your own private box which can be used in a number of ways.

1   You may come across a thought while going through this book that you want to hang on to, then carry it forward and put it in this box and reinforce it in your own mind

2   As a purchaser of 365 days of Inspiration you will be receiving a regular newsletter giving you more inspirational thoughts. Here's where you can record them and reinforce them

3   You may wish to record other goals achieved, other thoughts gathered

HERE'S YOUR OPPORTUNITY

So it is now time to **start your journey** of

365 days of Inspiration

With 730 inspirational thoughts

A goal a day

An affirmation a day

Acknowledging your successes (over 1800) over the 365 days

More FREE inspiration by regular email to strengthen YOU

By the way, don't default on this journey. YOU deserve to unlock the inspiration from within YOURSELF and from the 365 days.

Best Wishes
David Salmon

Your 365 days of Inspiration

Day 1	Day 2
Morning inspirational thought **Expectations tie stones round the soul of your dreams** *Sarah Banbreathnac*	Morning inspirational thought **Life is a blank canvas; it is you who adds the colour. Make sure you aren't colour blind**
My goal for today is	My goal for today is
My affirmation for today is	My affirmation for today is
My successes for today have been 1. 2. 3. 4. 5.	My successes for today have been 1. 2. 3. 4. 5.
Evening inspirational thought **Although the past often plays a role in most peoples lives, it is how we adjust to it in the present that is the key**	Evening inspirational thought **Never talk defeat. Use words like hope, belief, faith, victory**
More food for thought	More food for thought

Day 3	Day 4
Morning inspirational thought **Security is about hanging on to what you've got and not letting go. Success is about taking risks and moving on and striving for new things**	Morning inspirational thought **One of the greatest human assets is our ability to rise to the occasion. Instead of questioning your ability to do anything, understand that you could if you had to**
My goal for today is	My goal for today is
My affirmation for today is	My affirmation for today is
My successes for today have been 1. 2. 3. 4. 5.	My successes for today have been 1. 2. 3. 4. 5.
Evening inspirational thought **There is a simple law of physics that states that things in motion tend to stay in motion and things at rest tend to stay at rest. So once you begin to pursue a goal, don't stop**	Evening inspirational thought **Your own determination may be a threat to others if you're attempting something they were unable or too afraid to do themselves**
More food for thought	More food for thought

Day 5	Day 6
Morning inspirational thought **Wallowing in your own self-pity is like riding an exercise bike. It uses up a lot of energy and gives you something to occupy your time but it doesn't get you anywhere**	Morning inspirational thought **Things don't happen to us, what we do with them happens to us**
My goal for today is	My goal for today is
My affirmation for today is	My affirmation for today is
My successes for today have been 1. 2. 3. 4. 5.	My successes for today have been 1. 2. 3. 4. 5.
Evening inspirational thought **Limiting beliefs are detrimental to us, the worst of all being the belief that we have limits**	Evening inspirational thought **Consider your life story that is always being written and rewritten with new characters entering and leaving the story daily. As the editor you have exclusive say in where the story goes**
More food for thought	More food for thought

Day 7	Day 8
Morning inspirational thought **Growth is a result of adjustments to changes in your circumstances**	Morning inspirational thought **Every time you "get it wrong" you increase the odds to "get it right"**
My goal for today is	My goal for today is
My affirmation for today is	My affirmation for today is
My successes for today have been 1. 2. 3. 4. 5.	My successes for today have been 1. 2. 3. 4. 5.
Evening inspirational thought **If Thomas Edison can take us from candle to light bulb and the Wright Brothers from ground to flight, then clearly your ability to create anything and everything you want is limited only by your imagination and tenacity**	Evening inspirational thought **Our lives can only become whatever our current beliefs or attitudes allow us to conceive for ourselves**
More food for thought	More food for thought

Day 9	Day 10
Morning inspirational thought **The more of your mind you give away, the less of yourself there is for you to use to reach your goals, because you give someone else too many of the strings to pull**	Morning inspirational thought **Criticisms are opinions belonging to others so don't take what isn't yours**
My goal for today is	My goal for today is
My affirmation for today is	My affirmation for today is
My successes for today have been 1. 2. 3. 4. 5.	My successes for today have been 1. 2. 3. 4. 5.
Evening inspirational thought **If I am kind to someone and they treat me like rubbish then I made my choice of what I would bring to that situation and they made theirs**	Evening inspirational thought **The only things that we truly possess are our experiences and our memories of them**
More food for thought	More food for thought

Day 11	Day 12
Morning inspirational thought **I will never be an expert in this life because my life is a work in progress**	Morning inspirational thought **I will always remember to learn and grow and never be corrupted by what I think I know**
My goal for today is	My goal for today is
My affirmation for today is	My affirmation for today is
My successes for today have been 1. 2. 3. 4. 5.	My successes for today have been 1. 2. 3. 4. 5.
Evening inspirational thought **Walking the path of life successfully begins with a simple technique - put one foot in front of the other and do it with confidence**	Evening inspirational thought **Being a leader in the direction of your own life often requires leaving behind those who won't follow**
More food for thought	More food for thought

Day 13	Day 14
Morning inspirational thought **It is good to have power, so long as it is the power to help**	Morning inspirational thought **Some people strive so hard to DO something remarkable that they forget it requires that you first BE something remarkable. Then the doing is easy**
My goal for today is	My goal for today is
My affirmation for today is	My affirmation for today is
My successes for today have been 1. 2. 3. 4. 5.	My successes for today have been 1. 2. 3. 4. 5.
Evening inspirational thought **Dreams are today's answers to tomorrows questions**	Evening inspirational thought **The only thing that sat its way to success was a hen**
More food for thought	More food for thought

Day 15	Day 16
Morning inspirational thought **When a quitter comes up with a really good reason why something won't work, a winner comes up with two reasons why it will**	Morning inspirational thought **In the story of your life are you a victim or a victor? It is the difference between being a recipient of life events and the initiator of them.**
My goal for today is	My goal for today is
My affirmation for today is	My affirmation for today is
My successes for today have been 1. 2. 3. 4. 5.	My successes for today have been 1. 2. 3. 4. 5.
Evening inspirational thought **Take care of the earth and she will take care of you**	Evening inspirational thought **Sometimes the poorest man leaves his children the richest inheritance**
More food for thought	More food for thought

Day 17	Day 18
Morning inspirational thought **We are limited but we can push back the borders of our limitations**	Morning inspirational thought **Hold yourself to a higher standard, but not so high that the fall would kill you**
My goal for today is	My goal for today is
My affirmation for today is	My affirmation for today is
My successes for today have been 1. 2. 3. 4. 5.	My successes for today have been 1. 2. 3. 4. 5.
Evening inspirational thought **Memory is the perfume of the soul** *George Sands*	Evening inspirational thought **Most of us don't fear failure as much as we dread getting blamed for it**
More food for thought	More food for thought

Day 19	Day 20
Morning inspirational thought **If you want to reach your goals, you have to fall and scrape your knees up a few times, This is the art of learning to walk**	Morning inspirational thought **There is no right - there is only right now**
My goal for today is	My goal for today is
My affirmation for today is	My affirmation for today is
My successes for today have been 1. 2. 3. 4. 5.	My successes for today have been 1. 2. 3. 4. 5.
Evening inspirational thought **The price of power is responsibility for the public good** *WW Aldrich*	Evening inspirational thought **Nobody makes a greater mistake than he who did nothing because he could only do a little** *Edmund Burke*
More food for thought	More food for thought

Day 21	Day 22
Morning inspirational thought **The more I learn, the more I have yet to learn**	Morning inspirational thought **There is more to life than what goes on between my ears**
My goal for today is	My goal for today is
My affirmation for today is	My affirmation for today is
My successes for today have been 1. 2. 3. 4. 5.	My successes for today have been 1. 2. 3. 4. 5.
Evening inspirational thought **The more you use your brain the more brain you will have to use** *George A Dorsey*	Evening inspirational thought **My best friend is the one who brings out the best in me** *Henry Ford*
More food for thought	More food for thought

Day 23	Day 24
Morning inspirational thought **The more I watch and learn from nature, the less I worry. No matter what problems I have in life everything still seems to be taken care of**	Morning inspirational thought **Just because you aren't doing it all doesn't mean you aren't doing enough**
My goal for today is	My goal for today is
My affirmation for today is	My affirmation for today is
My successes for today have been 1. 2. 3. 4. 5.	My successes for today have been 1. 2. 3. 4. 5.
Evening inspirational thought **The winds and the waves are always on the side of the ablest navigators** *Edward Gibbon*	Evening inspirational thought **Under everyone's hard shell is someone who wants to be appreciated and loved**
More food for thought	More food for thought

Day 25	Day 26
Morning inspirational thought **No one but me can determine what my actions will be. There is no one to blame for the conclusions I draw, the choices I make and the actions I take**	Morning inspirational thought **To get a degree improve your knowledge. To get an education improve yourself**
My goal for today is	My goal for today is
My affirmation for today is	My affirmation for today is
My successes for today have been 1. 2. 3. 4. 5.	My successes for today have been 1. 2. 3. 4. 5.
Evening inspirational thought **Our life is frittered away by detail. Simplify** *Henry Thoreau*	Evening inspirational thought **The significant problems we face cannot be solved at the same level of thinking we were at when we created them** *Albert Einstein*
More food for thought	More food for thought

Day 27	Day 28
Morning inspirational thought **The brain uses the eye to see the image but uses the heart to appreciate it**	Morning inspirational thought **All things begin and end with change, thus, no things begin and end. Change never ends, it is constant**
My goal for today is	My goal for today is
My affirmation for today is	My affirmation for today is
My successes for today have been 1. 2. 3. 4. 5.	My successes for today have been 1. 2. 3. 4. 5.
Evening inspirational thought **Friendships are fragile things, and require as much handling as any other fragile and precious thing**	Evening inspirational thought **Don't say a thing is impossible when it is only difficult**
More food for thought	More food for thought

Day 29	Day 30
Morning inspirational thought **The question in life is not whether you get knocked down. You will. The question is are you ready to get back up and fight for what you believe in?**	Morning inspirational thought **You'll get much further in life being wrong on occasion than you ever will by always trying to be right**
My goal for today is	My goal for today is
My affirmation for today is	My affirmation for today is
My successes for today have been 1. 2. 3. 4. 5.	My successes for today have been 1. 2. 3. 4. 5.
Evening inspirational thought **Moving fast is not the same as going somewhere** <div align="right">*Robert Anthony*</div>	Evening inspirational thought **The most important thing in communication is to hear what isn't being said**
More food for thought	More food for thought

Well Done.

You have reached the first 30 days.

You have now received 60 inspirational quotes

Have you created you affirmations?

Are you using them?

Are you saying them out loud at least ten times a day?

You should have recorded 150 successes.

No matter how large or small please acknowledge them and keep reminding yourself by looking back.

Are you receiving our inspiration newsletter with more inspiration?

Well, no time for a pit stop...

Time to continue to inspire yourself!

Day 31	Day 32
Morning inspirational thought **Life is a team event where each player makes up his own rules**	Morning inspirational thought **Be as tough as leather, strong but flexible**
My goal for today is	My goal for today is
My affirmation for today is	My affirmation for today is
My successes for today have been 1. 2. 3. 4. 5.	My successes for today have been 1. 2. 3. 4. 5.
Evening inspirational thought **Have a heart that never hardens, and a temper that never tires, and a touch that never hurts** *Charles Dickens*	Evening inspirational thought **You miss 100% of the shots you never take** *Wayne Gretzky*
More food for thought	More food for thought

Day 33	Day 34
Morning inspirational thought **Be narrow in your focus but wide in your vision**	Morning inspirational thought **Finding those special people in life is like panning for gold, you may spend years finding nothing more than dirt and rock, but one day you find the golden nugget you've been looking for, making the entire journey worthwhile**
My goal for today is	My goal for today is
My affirmation for today is	My affirmation for today is
My successes for today have been 1. 2. 3. 4. 5.	My successes for today have been 1. 2. 3. 4. 5.
Evening inspirational thought **Sometimes all a person needs is a hand to hold and a heart to understand**	Evening inspirational thought **Vision is the art of seeing things invisible** *Jonathan Swift*
More food for thought	More food for thought

Day 35	Day 36
Morning inspirational thought **It's the believers and risk takers who've made the world what it is**	Morning inspirational thought **We all have dreams but until we take action to realise them we have no chance of living the life our heart and mind have showed us is right for us. So dream, dare, act and live fully**
My goal for today is	My goal for today is
My affirmation for today is	My affirmation for today is
My successes for today have been 1. 2. 3. 4. 5.	My successes for today have been 1. 2. 3. 4. 5.
Evening inspirational thought **To see a thing once is better than hearing about it often**	Evening inspirational thought **Regret is an appalling waste of energy. You can't build on it, it's only good for wallowing in** *K Mansfield*
More food for thought	More food for thought

Day 37	Day 38
Morning inspirational thought **If you want more meaning in your life, then get off your butt and make some. When you run out make some more**	Morning inspirational thought **Doubt closes your eyes and darkens them to the possibilities. Hope opens them up again**
My goal for today is	My goal for today is
My affirmation for today is	My affirmation for today is
My successes for today have been 1. 2. 3. 4. 5.	My successes for today have been 1. 2. 3. 4. 5.
Evening inspirational thought **Nothing is as simple as we hope it will be**	Evening inspirational thought **In any controversy, the instant we feel anger we have already ceased striving for truth and have begun striving for ourselves**
More food for thought	More food for thought

Day 39	Day 40
Morning inspirational thought **A diploma is a measure of time, not of education**	Morning inspirational thought **Endings never come, but transitions and new beginnings are abundantly available**
My goal for today is	My goal for today is
My affirmation for today is	My affirmation for today is
My successes for today have been 1. 2. 3. 4. 5.	My successes for today have been 1. 2. 3. 4. 5.
Evening inspirational thought **There are substitutes for almost everything except work and sleep**	Evening inspirational thought **The effect of one upright individual is incalculable** *Oscar Arias*
More food for thought	More food for thought

Day 41	Day 42
Morning inspirational thought **There are no obstacles, only building blocks**	Morning inspirational thought **When life gives you horse crap, make fertiliser and grow a garden**
My goal for today is	My goal for today is
My affirmation for today is	My affirmation for today is
My successes for today have been 1. 2. 3. 4. 5.	My successes for today have been 1. 2. 3. 4. 5.
Evening inspirational thought **People who throw kisses are hopelessly lazy** *Bob Hope*	Evening inspirational thought **Beauty is not caused. It is** *Emily Dickinson*
More food for thought	More food for thought

Day 43	Day 44
Morning inspirational thought **Resisting change is like resisting breathing, breathing requires change, so change is what life is made of**	Morning inspirational thought **Try to succeed and you will fail, because trying is a half hearted effort. Either do whatever it takes or do nothing**
My goal for today is	My goal for today is
My affirmation for today is	My affirmation for today is
My successes for today have been 1. 2. 3. 4. 5.	My successes for today have been 1. 2. 3. 4. 5.
Evening inspirational thought **The world is all gates, all opportunities, strings of tension waiting to be struck** *Ralph Waldo Emmerson*	Evening inspirational thought **There is nothing in a caterpillar that tells you it's going to be a butterfly** *Buckminster Fuller*
More food for thought	More food for thought

Day 45	Day 46
Morning inspirational thought **Some people are useless, they are the ones who don't make use of themselves**	Morning inspirational thought **The value of a gift is unknown until you look inside the package. A person is no different**
My goal for today is	My goal for today is
My affirmation for today is	My affirmation for today is
My successes for today have been 1. 2. 3. 4. 5.	My successes for today have been 1. 2. 3. 4. 5.
Evening inspirational thought **No matter how serious your life requires you to be, everyone needs a friend to act stupid with**	Evening inspirational thought **No person is worth their salt until they have lost and won battles for a principle** *J Marsh*
More food for thought	More food for thought

Day 47	Day 48
Morning inspirational thought **Winning is the opposite to quitting**	Morning inspirational thought **Win to celebrate your own success, not the other persons defeat**
My goal for today is	My goal for today is
My affirmation for today is	My affirmation for today is
My successes for today have been 1. 2. 3. 4. 5.	My successes for today have been 1. 2. 3. 4. 5.
Evening inspirational thought **Ignorant is for now, but stupid is for ever**	Evening inspirational thought **Criticism is something you can avoid by saying nothing, doing nothing, and being nothing**
More food for thought	More food for thought

Day 49	Day 50
Morning inspirational thought **Knowledge without wisdom is as useful as a car without wheels**	Morning inspirational thought **Youth is wasted when one prefers old thinking to new ideas**
My goal for today is	My goal for today is
My affirmation for today is	My affirmation for today is
My successes for today have been 1. 2. 3. 4. 5.	My successes for today have been 1. 2. 3. 4. 5.
Evening inspirational thought **A friend may well be reckoned the masterpiece of nature** *Ralph Waldo Emmerson*	Evening inspirational thought **Fools grow without watering** *Thomas Fuller*
More food for thought	More food for thought

Day 51	Day 52
Morning inspirational thought **Be sure your zeal revolves around the importance of the cause, not the importance of having it**	Morning inspirational thought **People will line up to discourage you, but when those that will support you show up, it makes all the difference in the world**
My goal for today is	My goal for today is
My affirmation for today is	My affirmation for today is
My successes for today have been 1. 2. 3. 4. 5.	My successes for today have been 1. 2. 3. 4. 5.
Evening inspirational thought **I've learned that love, not time, heals all wounds**	Evening inspirational thought **When you are in love it shows**
More food for thought	More food for thought

Day 53	Day 54
Morning inspirational thought **People will only work as hard as their standards require them to**	Morning inspirational thought **Insist upon succeeding like you insist upon breathing, then nothing can stop you**
My goal for today is	My goal for today is
My affirmation for today is	My affirmation for today is
My successes for today have been 1. 2. 3. 4. 5.	My successes for today have been 1. 2. 3. 4. 5.
Evening inspirational thought **The optimist proclaims that we live in the best of all possible worlds. The pessimist fears that this is true** *James Branch Cabell*	Evening inspirational thought **There is only one thing in the world worse than being talked about, and that is not being talked about** *Oscar Wilde*
More food for thought	More food for thought

Day 55	Day 56
Morning inspirational thought **When you do something better than you did it the last time that is the definition of success**	Morning inspirational thought **Celebrate your successes great and small, you'll discover your successes outweigh your failures**
My goal for today is	My goal for today is
My affirmation for today is	My affirmation for today is
My successes for today have been 1. 2. 3. 4. 5.	My successes for today have been 1. 2. 3. 4. 5.
Evening inspirational thought **Evil is easily acquired, good is not** *Chinese Proverb*	Evening inspirational thought **A helping hand is worth more than a thousand words of advice**
More food for thought	More food for thought

Day 57	Day 58
Morning inspirational thought **f.e.a.r. is false evidence appearing real. When you're aim is success, make sure you're not focusing on the evidence against it**	Morning inspirational thought **People don't get what they deserve to get, they get what they go out and get**
My goal for today is	My goal for today is
My affirmation for today is	My affirmation for today is
My successes for today have been 1. 2. 3. 4. 5.	My successes for today have been 1. 2. 3. 4. 5.
Evening inspirational thought **The world is full of new initiatives to follow on from the old initiatives that didn't work** *Danielle Francesca*	Evening inspirational thought **One of the keys to happiness is a bad memory** *Rita Mae Brown*
More food for thought	More food for thought

Day 59	Day 60
Morning inspirational thought **Success begins when excuses end**	Morning inspirational thought **Success is a choice**
My goal for today is	My goal for today is
My affirmation for today is	My affirmation for today is
My successes for today have been 1. 2. 3. 4. 5.	My successes for today have been 1. 2. 3. 4. 5.
Evening inspirational thought **If you keep thinking about what you want to do or what you hope will happen, you don't do it, and it won't happen** *Joe DiMaggio*	Evening inspirational thought **Everyone you meet deserves to be greeted with a smile**
More food for thought	More food for thought

Congratulations you have made it to 60 days!

That means:

120 thoughts

300 successes – WOW - well done!

Which quotes appeal to you? Are you carrying them forward in the "more food for thought box"?

I hope that you are being nourished with inspiration.

You are now up to speed.

Day 61	Day 62
Morning inspirational thought **Success is like a scavenger hunt - you may have to visit many homes, but you inevitably find what you're looking for**	Morning inspirational thought **The exception to the rule is the doorway to success**
My goal for today is	My goal for today is
My affirmation for today is	My affirmation for today is
My successes for today have been 1. 2. 3. 4. 5.	My successes for today have been 1. 2. 3. 4. 5.
Evening inspirational thought **Those who can do, those who can't teach**	Evening inspirational thought **The past is a ghost, the future a dream and all we ever have is now** *Bill Cosby*
More food for thought	More food for thought

Day 63	Day 64
Morning inspirational thought **The ocean begins with a single drop of water, our dreams begin with the single decision to pursue them**	Morning inspirational thought **There are no impossibilities, only varying levels of difficulty**
My goal for today is	My goal for today is
My affirmation for today is	My affirmation for today is
My successes for today have been 1. 2. 3. 4. 5.	My successes for today have been 1. 2. 3. 4. 5.
Evening inspirational thought **One is never too old to unlearn bad habits** *Cees Buddingh*	Evening inspirational thought **Experience is something you can't buy in life**
More food for thought	More food for thought

Day 65	Day 66
Morning inspirational thought **Think only in terms of possibilities, never limitations**	Morning inspirational thought **You are no more than or less than anybody else is. You are only less than your full potential, thus capable of becoming more than you are now**
My goal for today is	My goal for today is
My affirmation for today is	My affirmation for today is
My successes for today have been 1. 2. 3. 4. 5.	My successes for today have been 1. 2. 3. 4. 5.
Evening inspirational thought **Life is what happens to us while we are making plans**	Evening inspirational thought **Destiny is not a matter of chance it is a matter of choice, it is a thing to be waited for, it is a thing to be achieved** *William Jennings Bryan*
More food for thought	More food for thought

Day 67	Day 68
Morning inspirational thought **A problem is merely a solution waiting to happen**	Morning inspirational thought **A promise is only valid upon delivery**
My goal for today is	My goal for today is
My affirmation for today is	My affirmation for today is
My successes for today have been 1. 2. 3. 4. 5.	My successes for today have been 1. 2. 3. 4. 5.
Evening inspirational thought **It's kind of fun to do the impossible** *Walt Disney*	Evening inspirational thought **A great pleasure in life is doing what people say you cannot do** *Walter Gagehot*
More food for thought	More food for thought

Day 69	Day 70
Morning inspirational thought **Don't plan your future on other peoples promises, only on the promises you make to yourself**	Morning inspirational thought **I am responsible for who I am and what I do. The rest is none of my business**
My goal for today is	My goal for today is
My affirmation for today is	My affirmation for today is
My successes for today have been 1. 2. 3. 4. 5.	My successes for today have been 1. 2. 3. 4. 5.
Evening inspirational thought **Opportunities are never lost, someone will take the ones you miss**	Evening inspirational thought **People always call it luck when you've acted more sensibly than they have** *Anne Tyler*
More food for thought	More food for thought

Day 71	Day 72
Morning inspirational thought **If you make yourself a target, then don't complain when the arrow hits you**	Morning inspirational thought **Too many people have become financial millionaires while ending up spiritual paupers**
My goal for today is	My goal for today is
My affirmation for today is	My affirmation for today is
My successes for today have been 1. 2. 3. 4. 5.	My successes for today have been 1. 2. 3. 4. 5.
Evening inspirational thought **A traveller without observation is a bird without wings** *Mosilh Eddin Saadi*	Evening inspirational thought **To achieve what you want, you have to be stronger than those around you** *Benjamin Disraeli*
More food for thought	More food for thought

Day 73	Day 74
Morning inspirational thought **Obstacles are transparent, when you can see through them you can work through them**	Morning inspirational thought **Don't define yourself too narrowly, use a thesaurus**
My goal for today is	My goal for today is
My affirmation for today is	My affirmation for today is
My successes for today have been 1. 2. 3. 4. 5.	My successes for today have been 1. 2. 3. 4. 5.
Evening inspirational thought **Many mothers will do anything for their children except let them be themselves**	Evening inspirational thought **Laughter is a tranquilliser with no side effects**
More food for thought	More food for thought

Day 75	Day 76
Morning inspirational thought **I am three things - Who I was, Who I am, Who I am becoming**	Morning inspirational thought **If an acorn can grow into an oak tree, you can reach any goal. Like an acorn, all you require are the right circumstances and patience. After that it's just a matter of time**
My goal for today is	My goal for today is
My affirmation for today is	My affirmation for today is
My successes for today have been 1. 2. 3. 4. 5.	My successes for today have been 1. 2. 3. 4. 5.
Evening inspirational thought **Little things affect little minds** *Benjamin Disraelli*	Evening inspirational thought **We have two ears and one mouth so that we can listen twice as much as we speak** *Epictetus*
More food for thought	More food for thought

Day 77	Day 78
Morning inspirational thought **It isn't enough to have potential, you must maximise it**	Morning inspirational thought **Life is like a garden. Water the weeds and growth is difficult. Water the flowers and new blossoms appear over and over**
My goal for today is	My goal for today is
My affirmation for today is	My affirmation for today is
My successes for today have been 1. 2. 3. 4. 5.	My successes for today have been 1. 2. 3. 4. 5.
Evening inspirational thought **The conventional view serves to protect us from the painful job of thinking** *John Kenneth Galbraith*	Evening inspirational thought **When you harbour bitterness, happiness will dock elsewhere**
More food for thought	More food for thought

Day 79	Day 80
Morning inspirational thought **You are an Olympic hurdler. There are plenty of hurdles placed in your way as you pursue the finish line. Every single hurdle is part of the race and each one, when approached in the right way, can be overcome**	Morning inspirational thought **People can hand you opportunities, but nobody can hand you preparation**
My goal for today is	My goal for today is
My affirmation for today is	My affirmation for today is
My successes for today have been 1. 2. 3. 4. 5.	My successes for today have been 1. 2. 3. 4. 5.
Evening inspirational thought **To sit alone with my conscience will be judgement enough for me** *Charles William Stubbs*	Evening inspirational thought **Many complain of their looks, but none of their brains** *Yiddish Proverb*
More food for thought	More food for thought

Day 81	Day 82
Morning inspirational thought **You are your primary instrument, and you must be sharp. Blunt saws don't cut very well**	Morning inspirational thought **People who think big will never encourage you to think small, find them**
My goal for today is	My goal for today is
My affirmation for today is	My affirmation for today is
My successes for today have been 1. 2. 3. 4. 5.	My successes for today have been 1. 2. 3. 4. 5.
Evening inspirational thought **Consciousness is that annoying time between sleep**	Evening inspirational thought **Let not the opportunity pass for it may not return**
More food for thought	More food for thought

Day 83	Day 84
Morning inspirational thought **I am immortal, my body however is not**	Morning inspirational thought **If you want to be immortal live a life worth remembering**
My goal for today is	My goal for today is
My affirmation for today is	My affirmation for today is
My successes for today have been 1. 2. 3. 4. 5.	My successes for today have been 1. 2. 3. 4. 5.
Evening inspirational thought **It is easy to be tolerant when you don't care**	Evening inspirational thought **Blessed is he who expects nothing for he shall not be disappointed**
More food for thought	More food for thought

Day 85	Day 86
Morning inspirational thought **The only thing you can control in life is what you contribute to it**	Morning inspirational thought **Life is to be lived deliberately. If you're driven by habit you are asleep at the wheel**
My goal for today is	My goal for today is
My affirmation for today is	My affirmation for today is
My successes for today have been 1. 2. 3. 4. 5.	My successes for today have been 1. 2. 3. 4. 5.
Evening inspirational thought **You will never find time for anything. If you want time, you must make it** *Charles Bixton*	Evening inspirational thought **If past history was all there was to the games, the richest people would be librarians** *Warren Buffett*
More food for thought	More food for thought

Day 87	Day 88
Morning inspirational thought **Life is a puzzle. Once you have the picture in mind find the pieces and put it together**	Morning inspirational thought **Life's purpose is discovered when each individual determines where their passion and ability meet**
My goal for today is	My goal for today is
My affirmation for today is	My affirmation for today is
My successes for today have been 1. 2. 3. 4. 5.	My successes for today have been 1. 2. 3. 4. 5.
Evening inspirational thought **You are never a loser until you quit trying** *Mike Ditka*	Evening inspirational thought **Be part of the answer, not part of the problem** *Buell Gallagher*
More food for thought	More food for thought

Day 89	Day 90
Morning inspirational thought **Living and painting are both art forms. First you imagine the image of what it can be, then you take the steps to create it**	Morning inspirational thought **No journey in life is worth taking if it doesn't leave you postmarked from the trip**
My goal for today is	My goal for today is
My affirmation for today is	My affirmation for today is
My successes for today have been 1. 2. 3. 4. 5.	My successes for today have been 1. 2. 3. 4. 5.
Evening inspirational thought **A smile is an inexpensive way to improve your looks**	Evening inspirational thought **The average person thinks he isn't** *Father Larry Lorenzoni*
More food for thought	More food for thought

I bet you can't believe it...

90 days have now been completed!

WOW, that's:

180 thoughts

450 successes

Plus more from the e mail newsletter!

If you have now completed all your pages you will now be fighting fit with inspiration.

If you have enjoyed the first 90 days just think what the future has in store for you.

Keep up the great work!

Day 91	Day 92
Morning inspirational thought **The more black and white I try to make life the greyer it seems to get**	Morning inspirational thought **It is impossible to say the wrong thing while listening**
My goal for today is	My goal for today is
My affirmation for today is	My affirmation for today is
My successes for today have been 1. 2. 3. 4. 5.	My successes for today have been 1. 2. 3. 4. 5.
Evening inspirational thought **People don't notice whether it's winter or summer when they're happy** *Anton Chekhov*	Evening inspirational thought **A perfect method for adding drama to life is to wait until the deadline looms large**
More food for thought	More food for thought

Day 93	Day 94
Morning inspirational thought **There are some whose passion in life is doing whatever it takes to make a buck. My passion in life is doing whatever it takes to make a difference**	Morning inspirational thought **Doing something successfully doesn't mean doing it perfectly**
My goal for today is	My goal for today is
My affirmation for today is	My affirmation for today is
My successes for today have been 1. 2. 3. 4. 5.	My successes for today have been 1. 2. 3. 4. 5.
Evening inspirational thought **Truth is often disguised in jest**	Evening inspirational thought **The best way to reduce waste is not to buy it in the first place**
More food for thought	More food for thought

Day 95	Day 96
Morning inspirational thought **The past is a place to visit but I wouldn't want to live there**	Morning inspirational thought **The past is done with us whether or not we are done with the past**
My goal for today is	My goal for today is
My affirmation for today is	My affirmation for today is
My successes for today have been 1. 2. 3. 4. 5.	My successes for today have been 1. 2. 3. 4. 5.
Evening inspirational thought **Life is like a mirror; if you frown at it, it will frown back, if you smile at it, it will return the greeting**	Evening inspirational thought **The more I want to get something done, the less I call it work** *Richard Bach*
More food for thought	More food for thought

Day 97	Day 98
Morning inspirational thought **Hope for a positive future is only prevented by clinging to a negative past**	Morning inspirational thought **Patience is only a virtue when it is tested**
My goal for today is	My goal for today is
My affirmation for today is	My affirmation for today is
My successes for today have been 1. 2. 3. 4. 5.	My successes for today have been 1. 2. 3. 4. 5.
Evening inspirational thought **No bird soars too high if he soars with his own wings** *William Blake*	Evening inspirational thought **A seed needs time, a little rain, and a little sun to become a great tree** *From 'A Bugs Life'*
More food for thought	More food for thought

Day 99	Day 100
Morning inspirational thought **People don't live in reality, they live in perception**	Morning inspirational thought **Do all you can, that's all you can do. As long as you see it all the way through**
My goal for today is	My goal for today is
My affirmation for today is	My affirmation for today is
My successes for today have been 1. 2. 3. 4. 5.	My successes for today have been 1. 2. 3. 4. 5.
Evening inspirational thought **An idiot will always talk a lot** *Sarah Fielding*	Evening inspirational thought **He who cannot forgive others destroys a bridge over which he must pass himself. For every man has a need to be forgiven** *Saint John Gaulberto*
More food for thought	More food for thought

Day 101	Day 102
Morning inspirational thought **A bird may be born to fly but that doesn't mean it has to get it right first time**	Morning inspirational thought **Hope is not a strategy**
My goal for today is	My goal for today is
My affirmation for today is	My affirmation for today is
My successes for today have been 1. 2. 3. 4. 5.	My successes for today have been 1. 2. 3. 4. 5.
Evening inspirational thought **The way to love anything is to realize that it might be lost** *G K Chesterton*	Evening inspirational thought **There are three ingredients in the good life - learning, earning, and yearning** *Christopher Morley*
More food for thought	More food for thought

Day 103	Day 104
Morning inspirational thought **Forgiveness is the sweetest revenge**	Morning inspirational thought **Only your real friends will tell you when your face is dirty**
My goal for today is	My goal for today is
My affirmation for today is	My affirmation for today is
My successes for today have been 1. 2. 3. 4. 5.	My successes for today have been 1. 2. 3. 4. 5.
Evening inspirational thought **Only those who adopt change survive** *Charles Darwin*	Evening inspirational thought **Don't marry the person you can live with, marry the person you can't live without** *Dr James Dobson*
More food for thought	More food for thought

Day 105	Day 106
Morning inspirational thought **Shared joy is double joy, shared sorrow is half a sorrow**	Morning inspirational thought **If opportunity doesn't knock, build a door**
My goal for today is	My goal for today is
My affirmation for today is	My affirmation for today is
My successes for today have been 1. 2. 3. 4. 5.	My successes for today have been 1. 2. 3. 4. 5.
Evening inspirational thought **Never confuse a single defeat with a final defeat** *F Scott Fitzgerald*	Evening inspirational thought **Don't be afraid to take a big step if one is indicated. You can't cross a chasm in two small jumps** *David Lloyd George*
More food for thought	More food for thought

Day 107	Day 108
Morning inspirational thought **Life's problems wouldn't be called hurdles if there wasn't a way to get over them**	Morning inspirational thought **What you don't see with your eyes, don't witness with your mouth**
My goal for today is	My goal for today is
My affirmation for today is	My affirmation for today is
My successes for today have been 1. 2. 3. 4. 5.	My successes for today have been 1. 2. 3. 4. 5.
Evening inspirational thought **The less time you have to work with the more things you get done**	Evening inspirational thought **Shallow people believe in luck. Strong people believe in cause and effect**
More food for thought	More food for thought

Day 109	Day 110
Morning inspirational thought **Friends are those rare people who ask "how are you?" and then wait for the answer**	Morning inspirational thought **Great ideas need landing gear as well as wings**
My goal for today is	My goal for today is
My affirmation for today is	My affirmation for today is
My successes for today have been 1. 2. 3. 4. 5.	My successes for today have been 1. 2. 3. 4. 5.
Evening inspirational thought **Some heights can only be reached by the heart**	Evening inspirational thought **Stubborn people make lawyers rich**
More food for thought	More food for thought

Day 111	Day 112
Morning inspirational thought **Don't let what you are unable to do get in the way of what you are able to do**	Morning inspirational thought **It is easier to believe than to deny. Our minds are naturally affirmative** *John Burroughs*
My goal for today is	My goal for today is
My affirmation for today is	My affirmation for today is
My successes for today have been 1. 2. 3. 4. 5.	My successes for today have been 1. 2. 3. 4. 5.
Evening inspirational thought **The greatest oak was once a little nut who held its ground**	Evening inspirational thought **Map out your future, but do it in pencil**
More food for thought	More food for thought

Day 113	Day 114
Morning inspirational thought **A rumour without a leg to stand on will get around some other way**	Morning inspirational thought **Always forgive your enemies, nothing annoys them so much**
My goal for today is	My goal for today is
My affirmation for today is	My affirmation for today is
My successes for today have been 1. 2. 3. 4. 5.	My successes for today have been 1. 2. 3. 4. 5.
Evening inspirational thought **Every job is a self portrait of the person who did it. Autograph your work with excellence**	Evening inspirational thought **Do not look to where you fell but to where you slipped**
More food for thought	More food for thought

Day 115	Day 116
Morning inspirational thought **Success is 10% inspiration, and 90% last minute changes**	Morning inspirational thought **There is no cosmetic for beauty like happiness**
My goal for today is	My goal for today is
My affirmation for today is	My affirmation for today is
My successes for today have been 1. 2. 3. 4. 5.	My successes for today have been 1. 2. 3. 4. 5.
Evening inspirational thought **Uncertainty and mystery are energies of life. Don't let them scare you unduly, for they keep boredom at bay and spark creativity** *R I Fitzhenry*	Evening inspirational thought **When wealth is lost nothing is lost, when health is lost something is lost, when character is lost all is lost**
More food for thought	More food for thought

Day 117	Day 118
Morning inspirational thought **Know your limits, but never stop trying to exceed them**	Morning inspirational thought **Gratitude is the best attitude**
My goal for today is	My goal for today is
My affirmation for today is	My affirmation for today is
My successes for today have been 1. 2. 3. 4. 5.	My successes for today have been 1. 2. 3. 4. 5.
Evening inspirational thought **Adversity is the foundation of virtue** *Japanese proverb*	Evening inspirational thought **Those with too much to say end up with too small an audience**
More food for thought	More food for thought

Day 119	Day 120
Morning inspirational thought **If you're going through hell, keep going**	Morning inspirational thought **The best way to cheer yourself up is to try to cheer somebody else up**
My goal for today is	My goal for today is
My affirmation for today is	My affirmation for today is
My successes for today have been 1. 2. 3. 4. 5.	My successes for today have been 1. 2. 3. 4. 5.
Evening inspirational thought **Don't be afraid to go out on a limb - that's where the fruit is**	Evening inspirational thought **"In closing" is always followed by the other half of the speech**
More food for thought	More food for thought

120 days!

You are doing a great job on yourself, by yourself.

Here's the numbers:

240 quotes - (Why not make a list of your favourites?)

Just think 600 successes - that is one fantastic achievement!

Congratulations!!!

When was the last time you acknowledged so many successes in your life?

How's the journey for you?

I hope that it is amazing!

Day 121	Day 122
Morning inspirational thought **For every minute you are angry, you lose sixty seconds of happiness**	Morning inspirational thought **Usefulness is happiness**
My goal for today is	My goal for today is
My affirmation for today is	My affirmation for today is
My successes for today have been 1. 2. 3. 4. 5.	My successes for today have been 1. 2. 3. 4. 5.
Evening inspirational thought **Ability will never catch up with the demand for it** *Malcolm Forbes*	Evening inspirational thought **Being kind is more important than being right**
More food for thought	More food for thought

Day 123	Day 124
Morning inspirational thought **Feeling gratitude and not expressing it is like wrapping a present and not giving it**	Morning inspirational thought **It's never too late to have a happy childhood**
My goal for today is	My goal for today is
My affirmation for today is	My affirmation for today is
My successes for today have been 1. 2. 3. 4. 5.	My successes for today have been 1. 2. 3. 4. 5.
Evening inspirational thought **Fear is that little darkroom where negatives are developed** *Marilyn Ferguson*	Evening inspirational thought **If fate throws a knife at you, there are two ways of catching it - by the blade or by the handle**
More food for thought	More food for thought

Day 125	Day 126
Morning inspirational thought **You cannot always have happiness, but you can always give happiness**	Morning inspirational thought **Act as if what you do makes a difference. It does**
My goal for today is	My goal for today is
My affirmation for today is	My affirmation for today is
My successes for today have been 1. 2. 3. 4. 5.	My successes for today have been 1. 2. 3. 4. 5.
Evening inspirational thought **One of the most labour saving inventions of today is tomorrow**	Evening inspirational thought **Friendships are far more easy to build, less costly than battleships and far more powerful** *Sir Harry Lauder*
More food for thought	More food for thought

Day 127	Day 128
Morning inspirational thought **If you can't feed a hundred people, then feed just one**	Morning inspirational thought **Wherever a man turns he can find someone who needs him**
My goal for today is	My goal for today is
My affirmation for today is	My affirmation for today is
My successes for today have been 1. 2. 3. 4. 5.	My successes for today have been 1. 2. 3. 4. 5.
Evening inspirational thought **Everything starts with yourself, with you making up your mind about what you're going to do with your life** *Tony Dorsett*	Evening inspirational thought **Education's purpose is to replace an empty mind with an open one** *Malcolm Forbes*
More food for thought	More food for thought

Day 129	Day 130
Morning inspirational thought **The true meaning of life is to plant trees under whose shade you do not expect to sit**	Morning inspirational thought **It's easy to make a buck. It's a lot tougher to make a difference**
My goal for today is	My goal for today is
My affirmation for today is	My affirmation for today is
My successes for today have been 1. 2. 3. 4. 5.	My successes for today have been 1. 2. 3. 4. 5.
Evening inspirational thought **There is more to life than increasing its speed** *Mahatma Ghandhi*	Evening inspirational thought **It's those small daily happenings that make life so spectacular**
More food for thought	More food for thought

Day 131	Day 132
Morning inspirational thought **Misery is almost the result of thinking**	Morning inspirational thought **Go the extra mile. It's never crowded**
My goal for today is	My goal for today is
My affirmation for today is	My affirmation for today is
My successes for today have been 1. 2. 3. 4. 5.	My successes for today have been 1. 2. 3. 4. 5.
Evening inspirational thought **Life is like a roll of toilet paper. The closer it gets to the end, the faster it goes**	Evening inspirational thought **Perfection is our goal. Excellence will be tolerated**
More food for thought	More food for thought

Day 133	Day 134
Morning inspirational thought **Improvement begins with I**	Morning inspirational thought **Instead of counting your days make your days count**
My goal for today is	My goal for today is
My affirmation for today is	My affirmation for today is
My successes for today have been 1. 2. 3. 4. 5.	My successes for today have been 1. 2. 3. 4. 5.
Evening inspirational thought **If at first you don't succeed, try management**	Evening inspirational thought **War doesn't decide who is right or wrong, only who survives**
More food for thought	More food for thought

Day 135	Day 136
Morning inspirational thought **We learn from history that we do not learn anything from history**	Morning inspirational thought **A half truth is a whole lie**
My goal for today is	My goal for today is
My affirmation for today is	My affirmation for today is
My successes for today have been 1. 2. 3. 4. 5.	My successes for today have been 1. 2. 3. 4. 5.
Evening inspirational thought **Patience and perseverance have a magical effect before which difficulties disappear and obstacles vanish** *John Quincy Adams*	Evening inspirational thought **To grow old is to pass from passion to compassion** *Albert Camus*
More food for thought	More food for thought

Day 137	Day 138
Morning inspirational thought **Hope never abandons you, you abandon it**	Morning inspirational thought **Swallow your pride occasionally, its non fattening**
My goal for today is	My goal for today is
My affirmation for today is	My affirmation for today is
My successes for today have been 1. 2. 3. 4. 5.	My successes for today have been 1. 2. 3. 4. 5.
Evening inspirational thought **A happy person is not a person in a certain set of circumstances, but rather a person with a certain set of attitudes** *Hugh Downs*	Evening inspirational thought **When you plan to get even with someone you are only letting that person continue to hurt you**
More food for thought	More food for thought

Day 139	Day 140
Morning inspirational thought **When you stretch the truth watch out for the snap back**	Morning inspirational thought **A man wrapped up in himself makes a very small bundle**
My goal for today is	My goal for today is
My affirmation for today is	My affirmation for today is
My successes for today have been 1. 2. 3. 4. 5.	My successes for today have been 1. 2. 3. 4. 5.
Evening inspirational thought **Knowledge is created by the learner, not given by the teacher**	Evening inspirational thought **When people go to work they shouldn't have to leave their hearts at home**
More food for thought	More food for thought

Day 141	Day 142
Morning inspirational thought **Its always the secure who are humble; none are so empty as those who are full of themselves**	Morning inspirational thought **Flattery is all right so long as you don't inhale**
My goal for today is	My goal for today is
My affirmation for today is	My affirmation for today is
My successes for today have been 1. 2. 3. 4. 5.	My successes for today have been 1. 2. 3. 4. 5.
Evening inspirational thought **You can be 100% certain of being a success if you decide to go into fault finding**	Evening inspirational thought **Never put off until tomorrow what you can avoid altogether**
More food for thought	More food for thought

Day 143	Day 144
Morning inspirational thought **Every survival kit should include a sense of humour**	Morning inspirational thought **People may doubt what you say but they will believe what you do**
My goal for today is	My goal for today is
My affirmation for today is	My affirmation for today is
My successes for today have been 1. 2. 3. 4. 5.	My successes for today have been 1. 2. 3. 4. 5.
Evening inspirational thought **The worst bankrupt in the world is the person who has lost his enthusiasm** *H W Arnold*	Evening inspirational thought **Beware the fury of a patient man** *John Dryden*
More food for thought	More food for thought

Day 145	Day 146
Morning inspirational thought **There are no rules of architecture for a castle in the sky**	Morning inspirational thought **When patterns are broken, new worlds emerge**
My goal for today is	My goal for today is
My affirmation for today is	My affirmation for today is
My successes for today have been 1. 2. 3. 4. 5.	My successes for today have been 1. 2. 3. 4. 5.
Evening inspirational thought **Liberty is always dangerous, but it is the safest thing we have** *Harry Emerson Fosdick*	Evening inspirational thought **When ideas fail, words come in very handy** *Goethe*
More food for thought	More food for thought

Day 147	Day 148
Morning inspirational thought **Wisdom is knowing what to do next, virtue is doing it**	Morning inspirational thought **Character is doing the right thing when nobody's looking**
My goal for today is	My goal for today is
My affirmation for today is	My affirmation for today is
My successes for today have been 1. 2. 3. 4. 5.	My successes for today have been 1. 2. 3. 4. 5.
Evening inspirational thought **I can't choose how I feel, but I can choose what I do about it**	Evening inspirational thought **Why is "abbreviation" such a long word?**
More food for thought	More food for thought

Day 149	Day 150
Morning inspirational thought **Try not to become a man of success, but rather try to become a man of value**	Morning inspirational thought **A man cannot be comfortable without his own approval**
My goal for today is	My goal for today is
My affirmation for today is	My affirmation for today is
My successes for today have been 1. 2. 3. 4. 5.	My successes for today have been 1. 2. 3. 4. 5.
Evening inspirational thought **Teamwork means never having to take all the blame yourself**	Evening inspirational thought **The wise man looks at all sides of the question. The petty man can see only one side** *Confucius*
More food for thought	More food for thought

150 days - Congratulations.

Almost half way.

Can you believe it?

300 – yes, 300 inspirational quotes

600 successes.

*Why not look back and highlight your top 10 or 20
successes and celebrate and treat yourself.
You deserve it!*

Just think how far you have travelled on this journey.

Day 151	Day 152
Morning inspirational thought **Goodness is the only investment that never fails**	Morning inspirational thought **The reputation of a thousand years may be determined by the conduct of one hour**
My goal for today is	My goal for today is
My affirmation for today is	My affirmation for today is
My successes for today have been 1. 2. 3. 4. 5.	My successes for today have been 1. 2. 3. 4. 5.
Evening inspirational thought **You're only here for about 650,000 hours so give it your best shot** *Ferg*	Evening inspirational thought **You will become as small as your controlling desire, as great as your dominant aspiration** *James Allen*
More food for thought	More food for thought

Day 153	Day 154
Morning inspirational thought **Men are not punished for their sins, but by them**	Morning inspirational thought **The time is always right to do what is right**
My goal for today is	My goal for today is
My affirmation for today is	My affirmation for today is
My successes for today have been 1. 2. 3. 4. 5.	My successes for today have been 1. 2. 3. 4. 5.
Evening inspirational thought **It is not real work unless you would rather be doing something else** *J M Barrie*	Evening inspirational thought **To invent you need a good imagination and a pile of junk** *Thomas A Edison*
More food for thought	More food for thought

Day 155	Day 156
Morning inspirational thought **Have a very good reason for everything that you do**	Morning inspirational thought **The optimist invents the aeroplane and the pessimist the parachute**
My goal for today is	My goal for today is
My affirmation for today is	My affirmation for today is
My successes for today have been 1. 2. 3. 4. 5.	My successes for today have been 1. 2. 3. 4. 5.
Evening inspirational thought **No man should judge unless he asks himself in absolute honesty whether in a similar situation he might not have done the same** *Viktor Frankl*	Evening inspirational thought **The greatest difficulties lie where we are not looking for them** *Goethe*
More food for thought	More food for thought

Day 157	Day 158
Morning inspirational thought **No one is perfect, that's why pencils have erasers**	Morning inspirational thought **The road to success is dotted with many tempting parking places**
My goal for today is	My goal for today is
My affirmation for today is	My affirmation for today is
My successes for today have been 1. 2. 3. 4. 5.	My successes for today have been 1. 2. 3. 4. 5.
Evening inspirational thought **It is best to give advice in only two circumstances, when it is requested and when it is a life threatening situation**	Evening inspirational thought **Don't let what you cannot do interfere with what you can do**
More food for thought	More food for thought

Day 159	Day 160
Morning inspirational thought **When your dreams turn to dust, vacuum**	Morning inspirational thought **Some people are so fond of ill luck that they run half way to meet it**
My goal for today is	My goal for today is
My affirmation for today is	My affirmation for today is
My successes for today have been 1. 2. 3. 4. 5.	My successes for today have been 1. 2. 3. 4. 5.
Evening inspirational thought **Kindness consists of loving people more than they deserve**	Evening inspirational thought **The more original a discovery, the more obvious it seems afterwards**
More food for thought	More food for thought

Day 161	Day 162
Morning inspirational thought **It doesn't hurt to be optimistic. You can always cry later**	Morning inspirational thought **Better a diamond with a flaw than a pebble without**
My goal for today is	My goal for today is
My affirmation for today is	My affirmation for today is
My successes for today have been 1. 2. 3. 4. 5.	My successes for today have been 1. 2. 3. 4. 5.
Evening inspirational thought **Don't be afraid of the space between your dreams and reality. If you can dream it, you can make it so** *Belva Davis*	Evening inspirational thought **He that lives upon hope will die fasting** *Benjamin Franklin*
More food for thought	More food for thought

Day 163	Day 164
Morning inspirational thought **Always borrow money from a pessimist - he doesn't expect to be paid back**	Morning inspirational thought **Big shots are only little shots who keep shooting**
My goal for today is	My goal for today is
My affirmation for today is	My affirmation for today is
My successes for today have been 1. 2. 3. 4. 5.	My successes for today have been 1. 2. 3. 4. 5.
Evening inspirational thought **Everyone wants to live on top of the mountain, but all the happiness and growth occurs while you're climbing it**	Evening inspirational thought **Be civil to all, sociable to many, familiar with few** *Benjamin Franklin*
More food for thought	More food for thought

Day 165	Day 166
Morning inspirational thought **When you aim for perfection you discover it's a moving target**	Morning inspirational thought **What we see depends mainly on what we look for**
My goal for today is	My goal for today is
My affirmation for today is	My affirmation for today is
My successes for today have been 1. 2. 3. 4. 5.	My successes for today have been 1. 2. 3. 4. 5.
Evening inspirational thought **A city is a large community where people are lonesome together**	Evening inspirational thought **Those who want much are always much in need** *Horace*
More food for thought	More food for thought

Day 167	Day 168
Morning inspirational thought **There is nothing good or bad but thinking makes it so**	Morning inspirational thought **Each moment is a place you've never been**
My goal for today is	My goal for today is
My affirmation for today is	My affirmation for today is
My successes for today have been 1. 2. 3. 4. 5.	My successes for today have been 1. 2. 3. 4. 5.
Evening inspirational thought **The only competition worthy of a wise man is with himself** *Washington Aliston*	Evening inspirational thought **The greatest weakness of most humans is their hesitancy to tell others how much they love them whilst they're still alive** *O A Battist*
More food for thought	More food for thought

Day 169	Day 170
Morning inspirational thought **Every exit is an entrance somewhere else**	Morning inspirational thought **Believe those who are seeking the truth. Doubt those who find it**
My goal for today is	My goal for today is
My affirmation for today is	My affirmation for today is
My successes for today have been 1. 2. 3. 4. 5.	My successes for today have been 1. 2. 3. 4. 5.
Evening inspirational thought **If the facts don't fit the theory, change the facts** *Albert Einstein*	Evening inspirational thought **I haven't failed. I've found 10,000 ways that won't work** *Benjamin Franklin*
More food for thought	More food for thought

Day 171	Day 172
Morning inspirational thought **Even a clock that does not work is right twice a day**	Morning inspirational thought **Don't miss the doughnut by looking though the hole**
My goal for today is	My goal for today is
My affirmation for today is	My affirmation for today is
My successes for today have been 1. 2. 3. 4. 5.	My successes for today have been 1. 2. 3. 4. 5.
Evening inspirational thought **One should keep their words both soft and tender, because tomorrow they may have to eat them**	Evening inspirational thought **In golf, as in life, it is the follow through that makes the difference**
More food for thought	More food for thought

Day 173	Day 174
Morning inspirational thought **Words are like maps, both can show you the way**	Morning inspirational thought **Do not seek to follow in the footsteps of the wise. Seek what they sought**
My goal for today is	My goal for today is
My affirmation for today is	My affirmation for today is
My successes for today have been 1. 2. 3. 4. 5.	My successes for today have been 1. 2. 3. 4. 5.
Evening inspirational thought **The greatest of all faults is to be conscious of none** *Thomas Carlyle*	Evening inspirational thought **Indecision is the key to flexibility**
More food for thought	More food for thought

Day 175	Day 176
Morning inspirational thought **Preconceived notions are the locks on the door to wisdom**	Morning inspirational thought **It is better to know some of the questions than all of the answers**
My goal for today is	My goal for today is
My affirmation for today is	My affirmation for today is
My successes for today have been 1. 2. 3. 4. 5.	My successes for today have been 1. 2. 3. 4. 5.
Evening inspirational thought **We are not bodies with souls, we are souls with bodies** *Kevin R Bean*	Evening inspirational thought **When a man stops trying to prove he is a man, he is a man** *D Talmadge Gosnell*
More food for thought	More food for thought

Day 177	Day 178
Morning inspirational thought **If only closed minds came with closed mouths**	Morning inspirational thought **If you judge people you have no time to love them**
My goal for today is	My goal for today is
My affirmation for today is	My affirmation for today is
My successes for today have been 1. 2. 3. 4. 5.	My successes for today have been 1. 2. 3. 4. 5.
Evening inspirational thought **Am I not destroying my enemies when I make friends of them?** *Abraham Lincoln*	Evening inspirational thought **Flattery is like chewing gum. Enjoy it but don't swallow it** *Hank Ketcham*
More food for thought	More food for thought

Day 179	Day 180
Morning inspirational thought **Everything you can imagine is real**	Morning inspirational thought **Take life in your own hands, and what happens? A terrible thing, no one is to blame**
My goal for today is	My goal for today is
My affirmation for today is	My affirmation for today is
My successes for today have been 1. 2. 3. 4. 5.	My successes for today have been 1. 2. 3. 4. 5.
Evening inspirational thought **Given the choice between two theories take the one which is funniest**	Evening inspirational thought **When you fish for love, bait with your heart**
More food for thought	More food for thought

I bet you can't believe it

Yes, you have achieved 180 days!

I am not going to apologise but there's no time for pit stops on this journey.

360 quotes so far and even more to come.

Are you getting the newsletter OK? I would welcome your feedback.

Day 181	Day 182
Morning inspirational thought **Those who are unwilling to invest in the future haven't earned one**	Morning inspirational thought **If there were dreams to sell what would you buy?**
My goal for today is	My goal for today is
My affirmation for today is	My affirmation for today is
My successes for today have been 1. 2. 3. 4. 5.	My successes for today have been 1. 2. 3. 4. 5.
Evening inspirational thought **A wise person does at once what a fool does at last. Both do the same thing, only at different times** *John Dalberg Acton*	Evening inspirational thought **I have learnt silence from the talkative, toleration from the intolerant and kindness from the unkind yet strangely I am ungrateful to these teachers** *Kahill Gibran*
More food for thought	More food for thought

Day 183	Day 184
Morning inspirational thought **Living at risk is jumping off the cliff and building your wings on the way down**	Morning inspirational thought **Those who flee temptation generally leave a forwarding address**
My goal for today is	My goal for today is
My affirmation for today is	My affirmation for today is
My successes for today have been 1. 2. 3. 4. 5.	My successes for today have been 1. 2. 3. 4. 5.
Evening inspirational thought **Religion is for security, Spirituality is for discovery**	Evening inspirational thought **Things never go wrong in life, they just go different**
More food for thought	More food for thought

Day 185	Day 186
Morning inspirational thought **The finest thing in the world is knowing how to belong to oneself**	Morning inspirational thought **When the heart speaks take good notes**
My goal for today is	My goal for today is
My affirmation for today is	My affirmation for today is
My successes for today have been 1. 2. 3. 4. 5.	My successes for today have been 1. 2. 3. 4. 5.
Evening inspirational thought **Your degree of success is the result of your degree of awareness. The more you are aware of the more you have at your disposal**	Evening inspirational thought **There is no negative or positive in the emotions that we feel. There is only the honest expression of the wounds we need to heal**
More food for thought	More food for thought

Day 187	Day 188
Morning inspirational thought **You have succeeded in life when all you really want is only what you really need**	Morning inspirational thought **What great thing would you attempt if you knew you could not fail**
My goal for today is	My goal for today is
My affirmation for today is	My affirmation for today is
My successes for today have been 1. 2. 3. 4. 5.	My successes for today have been 1. 2. 3. 4. 5.
Evening inspirational thought **You can never take back the consequences of your choices. So choose wisely**	Evening inspirational thought **Never look back with regret, only with gratitude**
More food for thought	More food for thought

Day 189	Day 190
Morning inspirational thought **The trouble with resisting temptation is it may never come your way again**	Morning inspirational thought **You'll never find peace of mind until you listen to your heart**
My goal for today is	My goal for today is
My affirmation for today is	My affirmation for today is
My successes for today have been 1. 2. 3. 4. 5.	My successes for today have been 1. 2. 3. 4. 5.
Evening inspirational thought **When the loss of those you love leaves a hole inside your heart you can fill the hole with memories to help the sorrow depart**	Evening inspirational thought **The more rocks in the river the slower the water moves**
More food for thought	More food for thought

Day 191	Day 192
Morning inspirational thought **You grow up the you have your first real laugh at yourself**	Morning inspirational thought **Before you put on a frown, make sure there are no smiles available**
My goal for today is	My goal for today is
My affirmation for today is	My affirmation for today is
My successes for today have been 1. 2. 3. 4. 5.	My successes for today have been 1. 2. 3. 4. 5.
Evening inspirational thought **You may be able to blame your parents for a lousy childhood, but you have only yourself to blame for a lousy adulthood**	Evening inspirational thought **Real change is when you see the same old things differently**
More food for thought	More food for thought

Day 193	Day 194
Morning inspirational thought **Most people want to be delivered from temptation but would like it to keep in touch**	Morning inspirational thought **Everyone smiles in the same language**
My goal for today is	My goal for today is
My affirmation for today is	My affirmation for today is
My successes for today have been 1. 2. 3. 4. 5.	My successes for today have been 1. 2. 3. 4. 5.
Evening inspirational thought **Treat yourself to a facelift. Smile**	Evening inspirational thought **Status is a gauge people use to measure what isn't important**
More food for thought	More food for thought

Day 195	Day 196
Morning inspirational thought **If you wouldn't write it and sign it, don't say it**	Morning inspirational thought **The difference between having a 1 out of 10 life and a 10 out of 10 life is a choice**
My goal for today is	My goal for today is
My affirmation for today is	My affirmation for today is
My successes for today have been 1. 2. 3. 4. 5.	My successes for today have been 1. 2. 3. 4. 5.
Evening inspirational thought **Do you listen with the same enthusiasm with which you speak?**	Evening inspirational thought **Eternity starts before you die**
More food for thought	More food for thought

Day 197	Day 198
Morning inspirational thought **Judge your success by what you had to give up in order to get it**	Morning inspirational thought **The easiest way to save face is to keep the lower half shut**
My goal for today is	My goal for today is
My affirmation for today is	My affirmation for today is
My successes for today have been 1. 2. 3. 4. 5.	My successes for today have been 1. 2. 3. 4. 5.
Evening inspirational thought **The part of you that notices how old or how young, how fat or how thin you are never changes**	Evening inspirational thought **You can't forget what you won't forgive**
More food for thought	More food for thought

Day 199	Day 200
Morning inspirational thought **Keep smiling. It makes people wonder what you've been up to**	Morning inspirational thought **Of those who say nothing, few are silent**
My goal for today is	My goal for today is
My affirmation for today is	My affirmation for today is
My successes for today have been 1. 2. 3. 4. 5.	My successes for today have been 1. 2. 3. 4. 5.
Evening inspirational thought **Grief has opened many a heart that happiness couldn't**	Evening inspirational thought **A comparison is a sophisticated judgement**
More food for thought	More food for thought

Day 201	Day 202
Morning inspirational thought **The time to relax is when you don't have time for it**	Morning inspirational thought **As you climb the ladder of success be sure it's leaning against the right building**
My goal for today is	My goal for today is
My affirmation for today is	My affirmation for today is
My successes for today have been 1. 2. 3. 4. 5.	My successes for today have been 1. 2. 3. 4. 5.
Evening inspirational thought **It is impossible to create pressure without resistance**	Evening inspirational thought **Possibility is the seed of the flower**
More food for thought	More food for thought

Day 203	Day 204
Morning inspirational thought **Some people get lost in thought because it's such unfamiliar territory**	Morning inspirational thought **A smile is a powerful weapon - you can even break ice with it**
My goal for today is	My goal for today is
My affirmation for today is	My affirmation for today is
My successes for today have been 1. 2. 3. 4. 5.	My successes for today have been 1. 2. 3. 4. 5.
Evening inspirational thought **Achievement is the amount of success you allow yourself**	Evening inspirational thought **You must carry what you won't let go**
More food for thought	More food for thought

Day 205	Day 206
Morning inspirational thought **The kindest word in all the world is the unkind word unsaid**	Morning inspirational thought **Success is how high you bounce when you hit bottom**
My goal for today is	My goal for today is
My affirmation for today is	My affirmation for today is
My successes for today have been 1. 2. 3. 4. 5.	My successes for today have been 1. 2. 3. 4. 5.
Evening inspirational thought **Confidence is not being without fear. It's not allowing it to control you**	Evening inspirational thought **Friendships holds people together when they are apart**
More food for thought	More food for thought

Day 207	Day 208
Morning inspirational thought **Happiness is an inside job**	Morning inspirational thought **Let not the sands of time get in your lunch**
My goal for today is	My goal for today is
My affirmation for today is	My affirmation for today is
My successes for today have been 1. 2. 3. 4. 5.	My successes for today have been 1. 2. 3. 4. 5.
Evening inspirational thought **Peace. It doesn't happen to countries, only people.**	Evening inspirational thought **The reason many miss out is because their priorities are different to their dreams**
More food for thought	More food for thought

Day 209	Day 210
Morning inspirational thought **A child can ask questions that a wise man cannot answer**	Morning inspirational thought **Pick battles big enough to matter, small enough to win**
My goal for today is	My goal for today is
My affirmation for today is	My affirmation for today is
My successes for today have been 1. 2. 3. 4. 5.	My successes for today have been 1. 2. 3. 4. 5.
Evening inspirational thought **Personalities are fittings, not fixtures**	Evening inspirational thought **Try substituting the word excitement for the word fear**
More food for thought	More food for thought

210 days

What an achievement!

I bet you feel that you are climbing a mountain.

Just take a look back and congratulate yourself on your achievements and successes.

Just take a deep breath and recognise where you are right now.

Well Done!

Day 211	Day 212
Morning inspirational thought **Common sense is not so common**	Morning inspirational thought **The years teach much which the days never knew**
My goal for today is	My goal for today is
My affirmation for today is	My affirmation for today is
My successes for today have been 1. 2. 3. 4. 5.	My successes for today have been 1. 2. 3. 4. 5.
Evening inspirational thought **Whatever you blame will control you**	Evening inspirational thought **Many a life has been starved by the hunger for success**
More food for thought	More food for thought

Day 213	Day 214
Morning inspirational thought **Don't speak unless you can improve on the silence**	Morning inspirational thought **Always and never are two words you should always remember never to use**
My goal for today is	My goal for today is
My affirmation for today is	My affirmation for today is
My successes for today have been 1. 2. 3. 4. 5.	My successes for today have been 1. 2. 3. 4. 5.
Evening inspirational thought **How much do your opinions allow for the feelings of others?**	Evening inspirational thought **Sacrifice is the root of the flower**
More food for thought	More food for thought

Day 215	Day 216
Morning inspirational thought **Nature does not hurry, yet everything is accomplished**	Morning inspirational thought **The young man knows the rules, but the old man knows the exceptions**
My goal for today is	My goal for today is
My affirmation for today is	My affirmation for today is
My successes for today have been 1. 2. 3. 4. 5.	My successes for today have been 1. 2. 3. 4. 5.
Evening inspirational thought **The real art of listening is listening to those who will not listen to you**	Evening inspirational thought **The best place to have a party is between your ears**
More food for thought	More food for thought

Day 217	Day 218
Morning inspirational thought **Sometimes it's more important to be human than to have good taste**	Morning inspirational thought **Never ruin an apology with an excuse**
My goal for today is	My goal for today is
My affirmation for today is	My affirmation for today is
My successes for today have been 1. 2. 3. 4. 5.	My successes for today have been 1. 2. 3. 4. 5.
Evening inspirational thought **Selfishness will always be rewarded with discontentment**	Evening inspirational thought **Enjoy the dreams of others as well as those of your own**
More food for thought	More food for thought

Day 219	Day 220
Morning inspirational thought **Time is what prevents everything from happening at once**	Morning inspirational thought **Never explain. Your friends do not need it and your enemies will not believe you anyway**
My goal for today is	My goal for today is
My affirmation for today is	My affirmation for today is
My successes for today have been 1. 2. 3. 4. 5.	My successes for today have been 1. 2. 3. 4. 5.
Evening inspirational thought **Passion is the turbo boost on your life**	Evening inspirational thought **Use the past as a library, not a home**
More food for thought	More food for thought

Day 221	Day 222
Morning inspirational thought **Genius is nothing but a great aptitude for patience**	Morning inspirational thought **A hundred pound load of worry will not pay an ounce of debt**
My goal for today is	My goal for today is
My affirmation for today is	My affirmation for today is
My successes for today have been 1. 2. 3. 4. 5.	My successes for today have been 1. 2. 3. 4. 5.
Evening inspirational thought **Your self worth is measured by your ability to receive as much as your ability to give**	Evening inspirational thought **Happiness is a mood. Contentment is a state of being**
More food for thought	More food for thought

Day 223	Day 224
Morning inspirational thought **Envy slays itself by its own arrows**	Morning inspirational thought **The supreme accomplishment is to blur the line between work and play**
My goal for today is	My goal for today is
My affirmation for today is	My affirmation for today is
My successes for today have been 1. 2. 3. 4. 5.	My successes for today have been 1. 2. 3. 4. 5.
Evening inspirational thought **Every action marks the spot where a thought once stood**	Evening inspirational thought **Global amnesia would stop all wars**
More food for thought	More food for thought

Day 225	Day 226
Morning inspirational thought **I destroy my enemies when I make them my friends**	Morning inspirational thought **Trust yourself. You know more than you think you do**
My goal for today is	My goal for today is
My affirmation for today is	My affirmation for today is
My successes for today have been 1. 2. 3. 4. 5.	My successes for today have been 1. 2. 3. 4. 5.
Evening inspirational thought **Patience will always come to those who wait**	Evening inspirational thought **What do you hold onto the longest, a criticism or a compliment?**
More food for thought	More food for thought

Day 227	Day 228
Morning inspirational thought **It's nice to be important, but it's more important to be nice**	Morning inspirational thought **Troubles are a lot like people - they grow bigger if you nurse them**
My goal for today is	My goal for today is
My affirmation for today is	My affirmation for today is
My successes for today have been 1. 2. 3. 4. 5.	My successes for today have been 1. 2. 3. 4. 5.
Evening inspirational thought **Disappointment is simply a dream that doesn't want to become a reality**	Evening inspirational thought **You can't hold a hand whilst you're holding a grudge**
More food for thought	More food for thought

Day 229	Day 230
Morning inspirational thought **There is no greater loan than a sympathetic ear**	Morning inspirational thought **Don't wait for people to be friendly, show them how**
My goal for today is	My goal for today is
My affirmation for today is	My affirmation for today is
My successes for today have been 1. 2. 3. 4. 5.	My successes for today have been 1. 2. 3. 4. 5.
Evening inspirational thought **People who think they won't achieve much, rarely do. People who think they will achieve much, rarely don't**	Evening inspirational thought **Pain has created more love songs than happiness**
More food for thought	More food for thought

Day 231	Day 232
Morning inspirational thought **If you want to kill time, try working it to death**	Morning inspirational thought **Laughter is an instant vacation**
My goal for today is	My goal for today is
My affirmation for today is	My affirmation for today is
My successes for today have been 1. 2. 3. 4. 5.	My successes for today have been 1. 2. 3. 4. 5.
Evening inspirational thought **The one who whispers will draw people closer than the one who shouts**	Evening inspirational thought **Only your lack of trust will ever stop you letting go**
More food for thought	More food for thought

Day 233	Day 234
Morning inspirational thought **How much pain they have cost us, the evils which have never happened**	Morning inspirational thought **Envy is the art of counting the other fellow's blessings instead of your own**
My goal for today is	My goal for today is
My affirmation for today is	My affirmation for today is
My successes for today have been 1. 2. 3. 4. 5.	My successes for today have been 1. 2. 3. 4. 5.
Evening inspirational thought **Don't be obsessed to live as long as you can, but as well as you can**	Evening inspirational thought **Anger is a breeding ground for illness**
More food for thought	More food for thought

Day 235	Day 236
Morning inspirational thought **The most important trip you may take in life is meeting people halfway**	Morning inspirational thought **There are no traffic jams when you go the extra mile**
My goal for today is	My goal for today is
My affirmation for today is	My affirmation for today is
My successes for today have been 1. 2. 3. 4. 5.	My successes for today have been 1. 2. 3. 4. 5.
Evening inspirational thought **People who reach out will always touch more**	Evening inspirational thought **Much of the beauty of life is missed by people who are busy seeking the approval of others**
More food for thought	More food for thought

Day 237	Day 238
Morning inspirational thought **What soap is to the body, laughter is to the soul**	Morning inspirational thought **Be kind. Every one you meet is fighting a hard battle**
My goal for today is	My goal for today is
My affirmation for today is	My affirmation for today is
My successes for today have been 1. 2. 3. 4. 5.	My successes for today have been 1. 2. 3. 4. 5.
Evening inspirational thought **Pain gives birth to miracles. Ask any mother**	Evening inspirational thought **Increase your odds. Don't wait for what's around the corner. Go and look around as many as you can**
More food for thought	More food for thought

Day 239	Day 240
Morning inspirational thought **Laziness is nothing more than the habit of resting before you get tired**	Morning inspirational thought **Anyone who stops learning is old, whether at twenty or eighty**
My goal for today is	My goal for today is
My affirmation for today is	My affirmation for today is
My successes for today have been 1. 2. 3. 4. 5.	My successes for today have been 1. 2. 3. 4. 5.
Evening inspirational thought **You don't find treasure on the surface**	Evening inspirational thought **Laughter is the dance of the spirit**
More food for thought	More food for thought

At 240 days there is going to be no stopping you now.

You have nourished yourself with:

280 inspirational quotes

You are now able to look back on over 1200, yes, 1200 successes.

If you have reached this milestone I bet you feel great!

Feel the inspiration that you have within and enjoy.

Day 241	Day 242
Morning inspirational thought **A man isn't poor if he can still laugh**	Morning inspirational thought **Life is short, but there is always time for courtesy**
My goal for today is	My goal for today is
My affirmation for today is	My affirmation for today is
My successes for today have been 1. 2. 3. 4. 5.	My successes for today have been 1. 2. 3. 4. 5.
Evening inspirational thought **Why should anyone like you, if you don't?**	Evening inspirational thought **You can grow big and strong without eating meat. Ask any tree**
More food for thought	More food for thought

Day 243	Day 244
Morning inspirational thought **The more sympathy you give, the less you need**	Morning inspirational thought **It's what you learn after you know it all that counts**
My goal for today is	My goal for today is
My affirmation for today is	My affirmation for today is
My successes for today have been 1. 2. 3. 4. 5.	My successes for today have been 1. 2. 3. 4. 5.
Evening inspirational thought **You can change what you see if you change how you look**	Evening inspirational thought **Do you listen or wait to talk?**
More food for thought	More food for thought

Day 245	Day 246
Morning inspirational thought **Life is simple, it's just not easy**	Morning inspirational thought **In spite of the cost of living, it's still popular**
My goal for today is	My goal for today is
My affirmation for today is	My affirmation for today is
My successes for today have been 1. 2. 3. 4. 5.	My successes for today have been 1. 2. 3. 4. 5.
Evening inspirational thought **The imagination is a dream factory of which realities are a by-product**	Evening inspirational thought **Fun is often traded for ambition**
More food for thought	More food for thought

Day 247	Day 248
Morning inspirational thought **There is no distance on this earth as far away as yesterday**	Morning inspirational thought **Who, when being loved, is poor**
My goal for today is	My goal for today is
My affirmation for today is	My affirmation for today is
My successes for today have been 1. 2. 3. 4. 5.	My successes for today have been 1. 2. 3. 4. 5.
Evening inspirational thought **Allow your words to pass first through your ears before allowing them out of your mouth**	Evening inspirational thought **It's the space between the walls which give the room its size**
More food for thought	More food for thought

Day 249	Day 250
Morning inspirational thought **Luck is what you have left over after you give it 100%**	Morning inspirational thought **Hospitality is making your guest feel at home, even if you wish they were**
My goal for today is	My goal for today is
My affirmation for today is	My affirmation for today is
My successes for today have been 1. 2. 3. 4. 5.	My successes for today have been 1. 2. 3. 4. 5.
Evening inspirational thought **All thoughts need your permission**	Evening inspirational thought **What if we've got it wrong and everything is right?**
More food for thought	More food for thought

Day 251	Day 252
Morning inspirational thought **The larger the island of knowledge, the longer the shoreline of wonder**	Morning inspirational thought **A life without cause is a life without effect**
My goal for today is	My goal for today is
My affirmation for today is	My affirmation for today is
My successes for today have been 1. 2. 3. 4. 5.	My successes for today have been 1. 2. 3. 4. 5.
Evening inspirational thought **You don't doubt there's a road just because it disappears around the bend and out of sight**	Evening inspirational thought **When I was young I thought I could change the world, now that I'm old I know I can**
More food for thought	More food for thought

Day 253	Day 254
Morning inspirational thought **No man is rich enough to buy back his past**	Morning inspirational thought **Love is a game that two can play and both win**
My goal for today is	My goal for today is
My affirmation for today is	My affirmation for today is
My successes for today have been 1. 2. 3. 4. 5.	My successes for today have been 1. 2. 3. 4. 5.
Evening inspirational thought **Life. Many people are too busy struggling with the stairs to notice there's a lift**	Evening inspirational thought **Gossip is an oral infection**
More food for thought	More food for thought

Day 255	Day 256
Morning inspirational thought **It wasn't raining when Noah built the ark**	Morning inspirational thought **Rudeness is the weak man's imitation of strength**
My goal for today is	My goal for today is
My affirmation for today is	My affirmation for today is
My successes for today have been 1. 2. 3. 4. 5.	My successes for today have been 1. 2. 3. 4. 5.
Evening inspirational thought **Forgiveness frees the forgiver, far more than the forgiven**	Evening inspirational thought **Inexperience often triumphs over experience because it doesn't know where to fail**
More food for thought	More food for thought

Day 257	Day 258
Morning inspirational thought **In the book of life the answers aren't in the back**	Morning inspirational thought **In skating over thin ice, safety is in our speed**
My goal for today is	My goal for today is
My affirmation for today is	My affirmation for today is
My successes for today have been 1. 2. 3. 4. 5.	My successes for today have been 1. 2. 3. 4. 5.
Evening inspirational thought **Don't devalue your life by not appreciating it**	Evening inspirational thought **Parents are responsible for your birth, not your life**
More food for thought	More food for thought

Day 259	Day 260
Morning inspirational thought **If you want to forget all your troubles wear too tight shoes**	Morning inspirational thought **We should give meaning to life, not wait for life to give us meaning**
My goal for today is	My goal for today is
My affirmation for today is	My affirmation for today is
My successes for today have been 1. 2. 3. 4. 5.	My successes for today have been 1. 2. 3. 4. 5.
Evening inspirational thought **Why allow harsh words to use your tongue**	Evening inspirational thought **Hypocrisy is invisible only to its user**
More food for thought	More food for thought

Day 261	Day 262
Morning inspirational thought **Think big thoughts but relish small pleasures**	Morning inspirational thought **Enjoy yourself, it's later than you think**
My goal for today is	My goal for today is
My affirmation for today is	My affirmation for today is
My successes for today have been 1. 2. 3. 4. 5.	My successes for today have been 1. 2. 3. 4. 5.
Evening inspirational thought **The measure of your greatest moment is its distance from your worst**	Evening inspirational thought **Until you change the same old problems will keep turning up wearing different clothes**
More food for thought	More food for thought

Day 263	Day 264
Morning inspirational thought **Get mad, then get over it**	Morning inspirational thought **The meaning of life is not an unquestionable answer, it is an unanswerable question**
My goal for today is	My goal for today is
My affirmation for today is	My affirmation for today is
My successes for today have been 1. 2. 3. 4. 5.	My successes for today have been 1. 2. 3. 4. 5.
Evening inspirational thought **The hardest arithmetic to master is that which enables us to count our blessings**	Evening inspirational thought **What matters is how it affects you, not how it is**
More food for thought	More food for thought

Day 265	Day 266
Morning inspirational thought **A man is not where he lives, but where he loves**	Morning inspirational thought **To is a gift. That's why we call it the present**
My goal for today is	My goal for today is
My affirmation for today is	My affirmation for today is
My successes for today have been 1. 2. 3. 4. 5.	My successes for today have been 1. 2. 3. 4. 5.
Evening inspirational thought **Prosperity is a by-product of persistence**	Evening inspirational thought **There are two ways to heaven. One is when you really die. The other when you really live**
More food for thought	More food for thought

Day 267	Day 268
Morning inspirational thought **Sarcasm is the sour cream of wit**	Morning inspirational thought **Don't let yesterday use up too much of today**
My goal for today is	My goal for today is
My affirmation for today is	My affirmation for today is
My successes for today have been 1. 2. 3. 4. 5.	My successes for today have been 1. 2. 3. 4. 5.
Evening inspirational thought **A healthy body is of little use to an unhealthy mind**	Evening inspirational thought **When you are unattached to the outcome there is no risk**
More food for thought	More food for thought

Day 269	Day 270
Morning inspirational thought **Forever is composed of nows**	Morning inspirational thought **People who are sensible about love are incapable of it**
My goal for today is	My goal for today is
My affirmation for today is	My affirmation for today is
My successes for today have been 1. 2. 3. 4. 5.	My successes for today have been 1. 2. 3. 4. 5.
Evening inspirational thought **Enthusiasm negates effort**	Evening inspirational thought **Time stops when you are doing what you love**
More food for thought	More food for thought

270 days

Don't forget you are your primary instrument, and you must keep sharp, blunt saws don't cut very well.

You have now experienced:

540 thoughts of inspiration

And achieved 1350 successes

By the way how are those affirmations?

Are you using them?

Day 271	Day 272
Morning inspirational thought **The only sure thing about luck is that it will change**	Morning inspirational thought **Adopt the pace of nature, her secret is patience**
My goal for today is	My goal for today is
My affirmation for today is	My affirmation for today is
My successes for today have been 1. 2. 3. 4. 5.	My successes for today have been 1. 2. 3. 4. 5.
Evening inspirational thought **How much you get from life will depend on your self worth, not your circumstances**	Evening inspirational thought **Real wealth is when you give your time to people, not sell it for money**
More food for thought	More food for thought

Day 273	Day 274
Morning inspirational thought **Nothing is worth more than this day**	Morning inspirational thought **Love is an irresistible desire to be irresistibly desired**
My goal for today is	My goal for today is
My affirmation for today is	My affirmation for today is
My successes for today have been 1. 2. 3. 4. 5.	My successes for today have been 1. 2. 3. 4. 5.
Evening inspirational thought **Wonderful things happen when you dare to dream outside of sleep**	Evening inspirational thought **Why wait to get out of life what you've put in, just enjoy putting in**
More food for thought	More food for thought

Day 275	Day 276
Morning inspirational thought **The only thing that overcomes hard luck is hard work**	Morning inspirational thought **Freedom is nothing else but a chance to be better**
My goal for today is	My goal for today is
My affirmation for today is	My affirmation for today is
My successes for today have been 1. 2. 3. 4. 5.	My successes for today have been 1. 2. 3. 4. 5.
Evening inspirational thought **Stubbornness has caused many a soul to miss the song**	Evening inspirational thought **With every breath comes the opportunity to see something differently**
More food for thought	More food for thought

Day 277	Day 278
Morning inspirational thought **You can't run away from trouble. There ain't no place that far**	Morning inspirational thought **In to already walks tomorrow**
My goal for today is	My goal for today is
My affirmation for today is	My affirmation for today is
My successes for today have been 1. 2. 3. 4. 5.	My successes for today have been 1. 2. 3. 4. 5.
Evening inspirational thought **Paradise is a consciousness, not a continent**	Evening inspirational thought **Maturity is growing wiser, not older**
More food for thought	More food for thought

Day 279	Day 280
Morning inspirational thought **Luck is when opportunity knocks and you answer**	Morning inspirational thought **The only real mistake is the one from which we learn nothing**
My goal for today is	My goal for today is
My affirmation for today is	My affirmation for today is
My successes for today have been 1. 2. 3. 4. 5.	My successes for today have been 1. 2. 3. 4. 5.
Evening inspirational thought **Never realise a dream until you have another to put in its place**	Evening inspirational thought **If you want an incentive to change your life, visit the future now, to see how it will be if you don't**
More food for thought	More food for thought

Day 281	Day 282
Morning inspirational thought **How can something bother you if you won't let it**	Morning inspirational thought **The darkest hour only has sixty minutes**
My goal for today is	My goal for today is
My affirmation for today is	My affirmation for today is
My successes for today have been 1. 2. 3. 4. 5.	My successes for today have been 1. 2. 3. 4. 5.
Evening inspirational thought **You may want to change, but are you ready?**	Evening inspirational thought **Making a living is rarely as rewarding as making a difference**
More food for thought	More food for thought

Day 283	Day 284
Morning inspirational thought **Problems are only opportunities with thorns on them**	Morning inspirational thought **Don't worry about avoiding temptation as you grow older, it starts avoiding you**
My goal for today is	My goal for today is
My affirmation for today is	My affirmation for today is
My successes for today have been 1. 2. 3. 4. 5.	My successes for today have been 1. 2. 3. 4. 5.
Evening inspirational thought **A breakdown is often the beginning of a breakthrough**	Evening inspirational thought **Only what you refuse to accept will ever be a problem**
More food for thought	More food for thought

Day 285	Day 286
Morning inspirational thought **Admit your errors before someone else exaggerates them**	Morning inspirational thought **There are people who have money and people who are rich**
My goal for today is	My goal for today is
My affirmation for today is	My affirmation for today is
My successes for today have been 1. 2. 3. 4. 5.	My successes for today have been 1. 2. 3. 4. 5.
Evening inspirational thought **Expanding on what is right instantly gives less space to what isn't**	Evening inspirational thought **Hanging on requires far more effort than letting go**
More food for thought	More food for thought

Day 287	Day 288
Morning inspirational thought **Smooth seas do not make skilful sailors**	Morning inspirational thought **From the errors of others, a wise man corrects his own**
My goal for today is	My goal for today is
My affirmation for today is	My affirmation for today is
My successes for today have been 1. 2. 3. 4. 5.	My successes for today have been 1. 2. 3. 4. 5.
Evening inspirational thought **Most people die without really living (don't be one of them)**	Evening inspirational thought **The only thing that can ever hurt you is your resistance to change**
More food for thought	More food for thought

Day 289	Day 290
Morning inspirational thought **We find comfort among those who agree with us, growth among those who don't**	Morning inspirational thought **A problem is a chance for you to do your best**
My goal for today is	My goal for today is
My affirmation for today is	My affirmation for today is
My successes for today have been 1. 2. 3. 4. 5.	My successes for today have been 1. 2. 3. 4. 5.
Evening inspirational thought **Your potential can never be measured or used up**	Evening inspirational thought **Enlightenment isn't switching on the light, it's seeing in the dark**
More food for thought	More food for thought

Day 291	Day 292
Morning inspirational thought **Age is an issue of mind over matter. If you don't mind, it doesn't matter**	Morning inspirational thought **He who angers you, conquers you**
My goal for today is	My goal for today is
My affirmation for today is	My affirmation for today is
My successes for today have been 1. 2. 3. 4. 5.	My successes for today have been 1. 2. 3. 4. 5.
Evening inspirational thought **Love… you can stop the flow from you, but never to you**	Evening inspirational thought **Fate may provide your journey. How you travel your journey is your choice.**
More food for thought	More food for thought

Day 293	Day 294
Morning inspirational thought **Do not regret growing older. It is a privilege denied to many**	Morning inspirational thought **Resentment is like taking poison and waiting for the other person to die**
My goal for today is	My goal for today is
My affirmation for today is	My affirmation for today is
My successes for today have been 1. 2. 3. 4. 5.	My successes for today have been 1. 2. 3. 4. 5.
Evening inspirational thought **Pain and pleasure. Thorns and petals of the same rose**	Evening inspirational thought **Good deeds get done, bad deeds get publicity**
More food for thought	More food for thought

Day 295	Day 296
Morning inspirational thought **If you love life, life will love you back**	Morning inspirational thought **He who trims himself to suit everyone will soon whittle himself away**
My goal for today is	My goal for today is
My affirmation for today is	My affirmation for today is
My successes for today have been 1. 2. 3. 4. 5.	My successes for today have been 1. 2. 3. 4. 5.
Evening inspirational thought **Excuses are the unlimited disguises of blame**	Evening inspirational thought **People, like caterpillars, think they'll never fly, and then one day**
More food for thought	More food for thought

Day 297	Day 298
Morning inspirational thought **The difficulties of life are intended to make us better, not bitter**	Morning inspirational thought **In giving advice seek to help, not to please, your friend**
My goal for today is	My goal for today is
My affirmation for today is	My affirmation for today is
My successes for today have been 1. 2. 3. 4. 5.	My successes for today have been 1. 2. 3. 4. 5.
Evening inspirational thought **Life's a jigsaw. We can get so wrapped up in trying to make the little pieces fit, that we miss the whole picture.**	Evening inspirational thought **Kindness has its own language**
More food for thought	More food for thought

Day 299	Day 300
Morning inspirational thought **Everyday may not be good but there's something good in every day**	Morning inspirational thought **Everything has beauty, but not everyone sees it**
My goal for today is	My goal for today is
My affirmation for today is	My affirmation for today is
My successes for today have been 1. 2. 3. 4. 5.	My successes for today have been 1. 2. 3. 4. 5.
Evening inspirational thought **Change a can't to a could and you've got a chance**	Evening inspirational thought **You don't have to own to appreciate**
More food for thought	More food for thought

300 days

A good round number.

You deserve to celebrate today.

You have achieved many great things.

You may be getting towards the end of the book but this is just the start of your journey...

Day 301	Day 302
Morning inspirational thought **Children need love, especially when they do not deserve it**	Morning inspirational thought **Only dead fish swim with the stream**
My goal for today is	My goal for today is
My affirmation for today is	My affirmation for today is
My successes for today have been 1. 2. 3. 4. 5.	My successes for today have been 1. 2. 3. 4. 5.
Evening inspirational thought **Each time you act on your imagination a thought gives birth. This is creation**	Evening inspirational thought **It may take a very big shake to wake you from a very deep sleep**
More food for thought	More food for thought

Day 303	Day 304
Morning inspirational thought **Fear has a large shadow, but he himself is small**	Morning inspirational thought **Try again. Fall again. Fail better**
My goal for today is	My goal for today is
My affirmation for today is	My affirmation for today is
My successes for today have been 1. 2. 3. 4. 5.	My successes for today have been 1. 2. 3. 4. 5.
Evening inspirational thought **Observers use others mistakes as their lessons**	Evening inspirational thought **You will find in others what you look for**
More food for thought	More food for thought

Day 305	Day 306
Morning inspirational thought **Old age isn't so bad when you consider the alternative**	Morning inspirational thought **The human spirit is stronger than anything that can happen to it**
My goal for today is	My goal for today is
My affirmation for today is	My affirmation for today is
My successes for today have been 1. 2. 3. 4. 5.	My successes for today have been 1. 2. 3. 4. 5.
Evening inspirational thought **Security is not having things, it's not wanting them**	Evening inspirational thought **If you applied what you knew, you'd be amazed at how much you know**
More food for thought	More food for thought

Day 307	Day 308
Morning inspirational thought **There is no cure for birth and death, save to enjoy the interval**	Morning inspirational thought **You can learn many things from children - how much patience you have for instance**
My goal for today is	My goal for today is
My affirmation for today is	My affirmation for today is
My successes for today have been 1. 2. 3. 4. 5.	My successes for today have been 1. 2. 3. 4. 5.
Evening inspirational thought **Jealousy - the inability to share in another's joy**	Evening inspirational thought **Accepting you've done your best can free you to go forward and do better**
More food for thought	More food for thought

Day 309	Day 310
Morning inspirational thought **Men do not quit playing because they grow old, they grow old because they quit playing**	Morning inspirational thought **Too many people miss the silver lining because they're expecting gold**
My goal for today is	My goal for today is
My affirmation for today is	My affirmation for today is
My successes for today have been 1. 2. 3. 4. 5.	My successes for today have been 1. 2. 3. 4. 5.
Evening inspirational thought **Greet criticism by asking, "How does that help me?"**	Evening inspirational thought **You will let go in death what you think you can't in life, so why wait?**
More food for thought	More food for thought

Day 311	Day 312
Morning inspirational thought **If you woke up breathing, congratulations! You have another chance**	Morning inspirational thought **Inside every older person is a younger person wondering what happened**
My goal for today is	My goal for today is
My affirmation for today is	My affirmation for today is
My successes for today have been 1. 2. 3. 4. 5.	My successes for today have been 1. 2. 3. 4. 5.
Evening inspirational thought **When a dream joins forces with an intention, the result is a reality**	Evening inspirational thought **A great place to meet is on equal terms**
More food for thought	More food for thought

Day 313	Day 314
Morning inspirational thought **Spend the afternoon. You can't take it with you**	Morning inspirational thought **All the so called "secrets of success" will not work unless you do**
My goal for today is	My goal for today is
My affirmation for today is	My affirmation for today is
My successes for today have been 1. 2. 3. 4. 5.	My successes for today have been 1. 2. 3. 4. 5.
Evening inspirational thought **Unconditional love is the flame of a candle, content to give its light to anyone**	Evening inspirational thought **Happiness can provide the music, but sadness can make you listen**
More food for thought	More food for thought

Day 315	Day 316
Morning inspirational thought **There are no passengers on Spaceship Earth. We are all crew**	Morning inspirational thought **Education is learning what you didn't even know you didn't even know**
My goal for today is	My goal for today is
My affirmation for today is	My affirmation for today is
My successes for today have been 1. 2. 3. 4. 5.	My successes for today have been 1. 2. 3. 4. 5.
Evening inspirational thought **A fear is totally dependant on one thing, you not wanting it**	Evening inspirational thought **A dream can steer you through a lifetime of realities**
More food for thought	More food for thought

Day 317	Day 318
Morning inspirational thought **Courage is being scared to death and saddling up anyway**	Morning inspirational thought **Never assume the obvious is true**
My goal for today is	My goal for today is
My affirmation for today is	My affirmation for today is
My successes for today have been 1. 2. 3. 4. 5.	My successes for today have been 1. 2. 3. 4. 5.
Evening inspirational thought **Why lend what you can afford to give?**	Evening inspirational thought **When someone wins, others lose. When someone leads, others follow**
More food for thought	More food for thought

Day 319	Day 320
Morning inspirational thought **You can't turn the clock back. But you can wind it up again**	Morning inspirational thought **If you obey all the rules you miss all the fun**
My goal for today is	My goal for today is
My affirmation for today is	My affirmation for today is
My successes for today have been 1. 2. 3. 4. 5.	My successes for today have been 1. 2. 3. 4. 5.
Evening inspirational thought **Remove the first letter of loneliness to find what is hidden within**	Evening inspirational thought **"Around the corner" holds fear for the pessimist and excitement for the optimist**
More food for thought	More food for thought

Day 321	Day 322
Morning inspirational thought **The future has a way of arriving unannounced**	Morning inspirational thought **Live every as if it were your last and then someday you'll be right**
My goal for today is	My goal for today is
My affirmation for today is	My affirmation for today is
My successes for today have been 1. 2. 3. 4. 5.	My successes for today have been 1. 2. 3. 4. 5.
Evening inspirational thought **Only what won't be given, can be taken**	Evening inspirational thought **When financial assets appreciate, they go up in value. The same happens with people**
More food for thought	More food for thought

Day 323	Day 324
Morning inspirational thought **He who buys what he does not need steals from himself**	Morning inspirational thought **As you grow older, you'll find the only things you regret are the things you didn't do**
My goal for today is	My goal for today is
My affirmation for today is	My affirmation for today is
My successes for today have been 1. 2. 3. 4. 5.	My successes for today have been 1. 2. 3. 4. 5.
Evening inspirational thought **Through your perceptions you can change anything**	Evening inspirational thought **The journey is the destination**
More food for thought	More food for thought

Day 325	Day 326
Morning inspirational thought **We never really grow up, we only learn how to act in public**	Morning inspirational thought **It is not the mountain that we conquer but ourselves**
My goal for today is	My goal for today is
My affirmation for today is	My affirmation for today is
My successes for today have been 1. 2. 3. 4. 5.	My successes for today have been 1. 2. 3. 4. 5.
Evening inspirational thought **Optimists have all the luck**	Evening inspirational thought **The most difficult relationship you will ever be in is the one with yourself - it's the one you can't walk out of**
More food for thought	More food for thought

Day 327	Day 328
Morning inspirational thought **Don't think you are on the right road just because it's a well beaten path**	Morning inspirational thought **The most damaging phrase in the language is "It's always been done that way"**
My goal for today is	My goal for today is
My affirmation for today is	My affirmation for today is
My successes for today have been 1. 2. 3. 4. 5.	My successes for today have been 1. 2. 3. 4. 5.
Evening inspirational thought **Remember you are pure love with skin on**	Evening inspirational thought **Happiness and sadness. Two tears that look the same but taste very different**
More food for thought	More food for thought

Day 329	Day 330
Morning inspirational thought **The trick is growing up without growing old**	Morning inspirational thought **The most exhausting thing in life is being insincere**
My goal for today is	My goal for today is
My affirmation for today is	My affirmation for today is
My successes for today have been 1. 2. 3. 4. 5.	My successes for today have been 1. 2. 3. 4. 5.
Evening inspirational thought **A scholar observing life sees an unwelcome outcome as a lesson. A victim sees it as just more bad luck!**	Evening inspirational thought **The optimist and the pessimist. Each produce a crop to satisfy their own appetite**
More food for thought	More food for thought

330 days

You are close to the end of this 365 day journey

But maintain the momentum....

Just look back for a while.

Can you believe it?

Day 331	Day 332
Morning inspirational thought **You will never find time for anything. If you want time you must make it**	Morning inspirational thought **Success comes in cans, not can'ts**
My goal for today is	My goal for today is
My affirmation for today is	My affirmation for today is
My successes for today have been 1. 2. 3. 4. 5.	My successes for today have been 1. 2. 3. 4. 5.
Evening inspirational thought **Constant analysis can cause paralysis**	Evening inspirational thought **Do you enjoy what might happen as much as you fear what might happen?**
More food for thought	More food for thought

Day 333	Day 334
Morning inspirational thought **Realize that true happiness lies within you. Waste no time and effort searching for peace and contentment and joy in the world outright. - Og Mundino**	Morning inspirational thought **The tragedy of life is not that it ends so soon, but that we wait so long to begin it**
My goal for today is	My goal for today is
My affirmation for today is	My affirmation for today is
My successes for today have been 1. 2. 3. 4. 5.	My successes for today have been 1. 2. 3. 4. 5.
Evening inspirational thought **As you work towards your goal, anxiously anticipating the light at the end of the tunnel, don't forget to notice the light that shines upon you today.** **Michelle Vrtuszeki**	Evening inspirational thought **When perseverance meets a good idea, it's only a matter of time**
More food for thought	More food for thought

Day 335	Day 336
Morning inspirational thought **Every day comes bearing its own gifts. Untie the ribbons**	Morning inspirational thought **If experience was so important we'd never have had anyone walk on the moon**
My goal for today is	My goal for today is
My affirmation for today is	My affirmation for today is
My successes for today have been 1. 2. 3. 4. 5.	My successes for today have been 1. 2. 3. 4. 5.
Evening inspirational thought **Eyes which look to darkness do not reflect the sun**	Evening inspirational thought **The quality control of your life is how you think. Everything must pass through it**
More food for thought	More food for thought

Day 337	Day 338
Morning inspirational thought **We do not inherit the earth from our ancestors, we borrow it from our children**	Morning inspirational thought **Dream as if you'll live forever. Live as if you'll die today**
My goal for today is	My goal for today is
My affirmation for today is	My affirmation for today is
My successes for today have been 1. 2. 3. 4. 5.	My successes for today have been 1. 2. 3. 4. 5.
Evening inspirational thought **Priorities are the creators of destinies**	Evening inspirational thought **Trust is letting go**
More food for thought	More food for thought

Day 339	Day 340
Morning inspirational thought **Small deeds done are better than great deeds planned**	Morning inspirational thought **Most of us spend our lives as if we had another one in the bank**
My goal for today is	My goal for today is
My affirmation for today is	My affirmation for today is
My successes for today have been 1. 2. 3. 4. 5.	My successes for today have been 1. 2. 3. 4. 5.
Evening inspirational thought **The only real victim of hatred is its creator**	Evening inspirational thought **What we give out is multiplied and returned. So watch what you give out!**
More food for thought	More food for thought

Day 341	Day 342
Morning inspirational thought **Confidence comes not from always being right but from not fearing to be wrong**	Morning inspirational thought **The best helping hand that you will ever receive is the one at the end of your own arm**
My goal for today is	My goal for today is
My affirmation for today is	My affirmation for today is
My successes for today have been 1. 2. 3. 4. 5.	My successes for today have been 1. 2. 3. 4. 5.
Evening inspirational thought **Blame is a prison which holds many victims**	Evening inspirational thought **Growing pains of the soul are often confused with a breaking heart**
More food for thought	More food for thought

Day 343	Day 344
Morning inspirational thought **It ain't what they call you, it's what you answer to**	Morning inspirational thought **Bravery is being the only one who knows you're afraid**
My goal for today is	My goal for today is
My affirmation for today is	My affirmation for today is
My successes for today have been 1. 2. 3. 4. 5.	My successes for today have been 1. 2. 3. 4. 5.
Evening inspirational thought **Confidence and ability are not related**	Evening inspirational thought **Emptiness is simply a lack of dreams**
More food for thought	More food for thought

Day 345	Day 346
Morning inspirational thought **Remember, no matter where you go, there you are**	Morning inspirational thought **If we did all the things we are capable of doing, we would literally astound ourselves**
My goal for today is	My goal for today is
My affirmation for today is	My affirmation for today is
My successes for today have been 1. 2. 3. 4. 5.	My successes for today have been 1. 2. 3. 4. 5.
Evening inspirational thought **God can't get through whilst the line is engaged**	Evening inspirational thought **Unconditional loving. That includes you**
More food for thought	More food for thought

Day 347	Day 348
Morning inspirational thought **The person who is waiting for something to turn up might start with their shirtsleeves**	Morning inspirational thought **It's not who you are that holds you back, it's who you think you are not**
My goal for today is	My goal for today is
My affirmation for today is	My affirmation for today is
My successes for today have been 1. 2. 3. 4. 5.	My successes for today have been 1. 2. 3. 4. 5.
Evening inspirational thought **Out of all the wonders in all the world the most incredible thing in your whole life, is already inside you.**	Evening inspirational thought **The past is like a field of grass, it looks greener from a distance**
More food for thought	More food for thought

Day 349	Day 350
Morning inspirational thought **Put your future in good hands - your own**	Morning inspirational thought **The best way to gain self confidence is to do what you are afraid to do**
My goal for today is	My goal for today is
My affirmation for today is	My affirmation for today is
My successes for today have been 1. 2. 3. 4. 5.	My successes for today have been 1. 2. 3. 4. 5.
Evening inspirational thought **Just follow the signs for desire as you drive away from the place called contentment**	Evening inspirational thought **Troubled waters can be crossed using a bridge called friendship**
More food for thought	More food for thought

Day 351	Day 352
Morning inspirational thought **Men are not against you, they are merely for themselves**	Morning inspirational thought **Faith is taking the first step even when you don't see the whole staircase**
My goal for today is	My goal for today is
My affirmation for today is	My affirmation for today is
My successes for today have been 1. 2. 3. 4. 5.	My successes for today have been 1. 2. 3. 4. 5.
Evening inspirational thought **"Learning more" can be a clever way to avoid applying what we already know**	Evening inspirational thought **Change can't be stopped but people try. We call this trauma**
More food for thought	More food for thought

Day 353	Day 354
Morning inspirational thought **There is no saint without a past and no sinner without a future**	Morning inspirational thought **One who walks in another's tracks leaves no footprints**
My goal for today is	My goal for today is
My affirmation for today is	My affirmation for today is
My successes for today have been 1. 2. 3. 4. 5.	My successes for today have been 1. 2. 3. 4. 5.
Evening inspirational thought **Sometimes people confuse a new opening in their life with a hole, and a great opportunity is missed**	Evening inspirational thought **The traveller needs to let go of each step along his journey**
More food for thought	More food for thought

Day 355	Day 356
Morning inspirational thought **A cynic knows the price of everything and the value of nothing**	Morning inspirational thought **Nothing ends, it only changes**
My goal for today is	My goal for today is
My affirmation for today is	My affirmation for today is
My successes for today have been 1. 2. 3. 4. 5.	My successes for today have been 1. 2. 3. 4. 5.
Evening inspirational thought **Progress and change. They have about as much in common as flame and fire**	Evening inspirational thought **Not to acknowledge your own greatness will simply deny it the right to exist**
More food for thought	More food for thought

Day 357	Day 358
Morning inspirational thought **Pain's love is fear. Pain's fear is love**	Morning inspirational thought **I know of a place where love, hope, forgiveness and so much more can be found, it's called a mirror**
My goal for today is	My goal for today is
My affirmation for today is	My affirmation for today is
My successes for today have been 1. 2. 3. 4. 5.	My successes for today have been 1. 2. 3. 4. 5.
Evening inspirational thought **To believe it, is ok To know it, is better To apply it, is best**	Evening inspirational thought **When anger is greeted with anger the result can only be more anger**
More food for thought	More food for thought

Day 359	Day 360
Morning inspirational thought **Why do so many find it easier to blame themselves for a wrong than to credit themselves for a right?**	Morning inspirational thought **Everything, but everything, other than love, is on loan**
My goal for today is	My goal for today is
My affirmation for today is	My affirmation for today is
My successes for today have been 1. 2. 3. 4. 5.	My successes for today have been 1. 2. 3. 4. 5.
Evening inspirational thought **You are the cause of your life not the effect of it**	Evening inspirational thought **No person is harder on us than we are on ourselves**
More food for thought	More food for thought

660 inspiration thoughts

1650 successes - no matter how large or small they all count!

Keep the affirmations going. If you have been saying just two affirmations a day since you started 10 times a day, that's 6600 reinforcing positive thoughts that you have given yourself.

That's great - you deserve it!

Day 361	Day 362
Morning inspirational thought **Your health is a physical manifestation of your thoughts, so make them good**	Morning inspirational thought **The foundations of your future are the memories of your past, if you only use the best ones the house you build will last**
My goal for today is	My goal for today is
My affirmation for today is	My affirmation for today is
My successes for today have been 1. 2. 3. 4. 5.	My successes for today have been 1. 2. 3. 4. 5.
Evening inspirational thought **Backward thinking people use their thoughts to examine their lives. Forward thinking people use their thoughts to create their lives**	Evening inspirational thought **Your thoughts create your actions, you create your thoughts**
More food for thought	More food for thought

Day 363	Day 364
Morning inspirational thought **All truly great people are known for what they gave, not what they got**	Morning inspirational thought **Stepping back isn't stepping off**
My goal for today is	My goal for today is
My affirmation for today is	My affirmation for today is
My successes for today have been 1. 2. 3. 4. 5.	My successes for today have been 1. 2. 3. 4. 5.
Evening inspirational thought **Being unhappy requires considerably more effort than being happy**	Evening inspirational thought **If you've taken for granted you've taken too much**
More food for thought	More food for thought

Day 365

Morning inspirational thought
**The greatest place to which you can
travel is the hearts of the needy**

My goal for today is

My affirmation for today is

My successes for today have been

1.

2.

3.

4.

5.

Evening inspirational thought
**In most cases the difference between a
do and a don't is a doubt**

More food for thought

365 days!

What an achievement!

How do you feel?

Just spend the next hour looking back on:

730 inspirational thoughts   (I hope that you have shared them with friends and family)

1825 successes

What an achiever you are!

Congratulations.

Have you been adding to your 365 days with your own thoughts and our email newsletter?

These 365 days may have finished but the journey continues.

Enjoy this road and where it is taking you.

Thank you

I hope that you found some of these quotes inspirational and you can carry them forward on a daily basis.

Well, until next time...

Best Wishes

David

Would you like another 365 days - just go to www.365daysofinspiration

Printed in the United Kingdom
by Lightning Source UK Ltd.
131670UK00001B/124-171/A